917.286  Carpenter, Allan
C
         Costa Rica

| DATE | | | |
|---|---|---|---|
| DEC 23 '92 | | | |
| MAR 24 | | | |

© THE BAKER & TAYLOR CO.

*Enchantment of Central America*

# COSTA RICA

by ALLAN CARPENTER

Consulting Editor
Professor Guillermo Segreda
Manhattanville College, New York

CHILDRENS PRESS, CHICAGO

**THE ENCHANTMENT OF SOUTH AND CENTRAL AMERICA**

Argentina, Bolivia, Brazil, British Honduras,
Chile, Colombia, Costa Rica, Ecuador, El Salvador,
French Guiana, Guatemala, Guyana, Honduras, Nicaragua,
Panama, Paraguay, Peru, Surinam, Uruguay, Venezuela

**ACKNOWLEDGMENTS**

His excellency José Joaquin Trejos Fernández, former president of Costa Rica; his excellency, Luis Demetrio Tinoco, ambassador of Costa Rica to the United States; William H. Rodgers, public affairs officer, United States Information Service, Foreign Service of the United States, San José, Costa Rica; Instituto Costarricense de Turismo, San José, Costa Rica; Costa Rica Travel Information Office, San Francisco, California; La Botija Artesania, San José, Costa Rica; Permanent Mission of Costa Rica to the United Nations, New York, New York; Kenneth C. Turner, Photograph Librarian, Pan American Union, Washington, D. C.

Map Artist: Eugene Derdeyn
Cover Photograph: Costa Rican oxcart, AVI Associates, Inc.
Frontispiece: Children's Park in San José, Pan American Union

Library of Congress Catalog Card Number: 71-157829
Copyright © 1971 by Regensteiner Publishing Enterprises, Inc.
All rights reserved. Printed in the U.S.A.
Published simultaneously in Canada

1 2 3 4 5 6 7 8 9 10 11 12 13 14 15 16 17 18 19 20 21 22 23 24 25 R 75 74 73 72 71

# Contents

A TRUE STORY TO SET THE SCENE .......................... 7
    Revealing the Culture of its People
THE FACE OF THE LAND .................................. 10
    Volcanic Salute—Features of the Face—Draining the Land—In Ancient Times—Climate
FOUR BOYS AND GIRLS OF COSTA RICA ...................... 16
    Sebastian of San José—Juan of Liberia—Negrita of Cartago—Minor of Limón—Four for All and All for Four
COSTA RICA YESTERDAY ................................. 29
    Ancient Costa Ricans—A Rich Coast—The Spanish Period—End of Spanish Rule—Time of Many Changes—A New Republic—The Case of William Walker—A Period of Growth
COSTA RICA TODAY ..................................... 41
    Modern Times—Distinguished Costa Ricans—The Government of Costa Rica—Education
NATURAL TREASURES ................................... 53
    Growing Things—Living Things—Minerals
THE PEOPLE LIVE IN COSTA RICA ......................... 57
    A "Different" Spanish Heritage—Where and How the People Live—Customs
THE PEOPLE WORK IN COSTA RICA ........................ 65
    Industrious Costa Ricans—Transportation—Water Transportation—Aviation—Highways—Railroads—Communications
ENCHANTMENT OF COSTA RICA ........................... 75
    Enchanting San José—Magnifico!—Pleasant City—Downtown San José—Cartago—Awesome Irazú—Other Central Plateau Cities—A Novel Train Ride—Puerto Limón—Other Points of Interest—Treasure Island
HANDY REFERENCE SECTION ............................. 90
    Instant Facts—Principal Cities—Provinces and Capitals—Fiestas and Fairs—You Have a Date with History—Spanish Pronunciation Guide
INDEX ................................................. 94

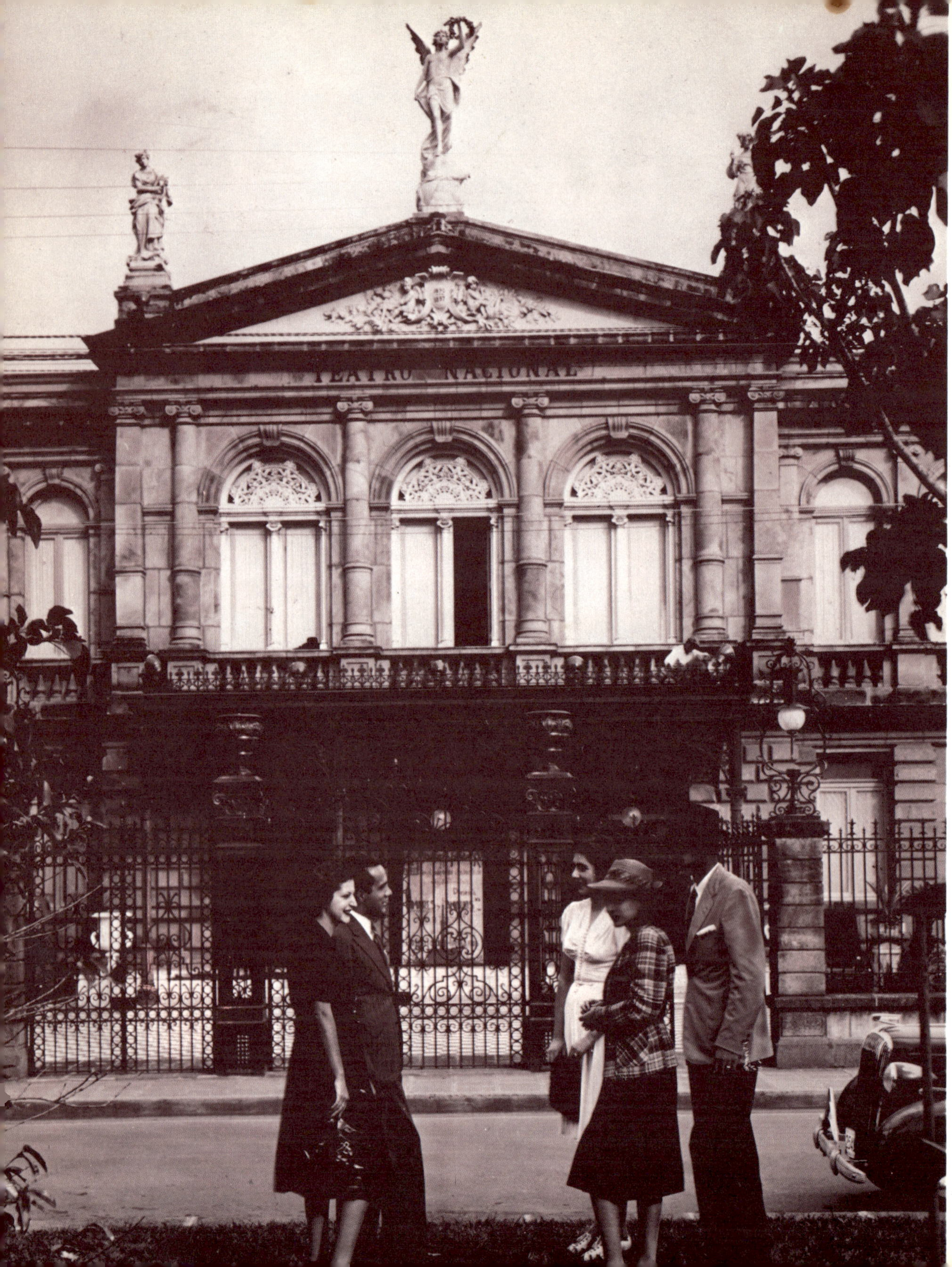
TEATRO NACIONAL

# A True Story to Set the Scene

**REVEALING THE CULTURE OF ITS PEOPLE**

The people chatted noisily as they approached the building, but once inside, the mood of the beautifully dressed throng changed to awe. As the crowd looked around at the magnificent interior, some even crossed themselves before a few of the marble statues.

Promptly at eight o'clock that evening the curtain went up in the beautiful main auditorium. Amid rapturous applause, Maestro Adeilhac led the orchestra in the national anthem; President Rafael Iglesias of Costa Rica and his family took their seats. The audience settled down as the great Paris Opera Company began its performance of the opera *Faust*.

It was a great day for Costa Rica—October 19, 1897. The triumphal event had its beginning in 1890, when an opera company headed by the famous singer Adelina Patti wanted to perform in San José, capital of Costa Rica. San José, however, had no building suitable for an opera performance.

The citizens were so disappointed and ashamed that a committee of merchants and other leaders prepared a plan: "The undersigned merchants and agriculturers, wishing that a theater be built for the rest and relaxation of the people, convinced

---

The National Theater in San José, Costa Rica, was opened on October 19, 1897, with a performance of the opera *Faust* by the Paris Opera Company.

**PAN AMERICAN UNION**

that a capital with a culture such as ours cannot be deprived of a center of this kind, and that the national income does not leave a surplus to be devoted to the execution of the work, do hereby offer to pay, for such purpose and for as long as it shall be necessary, five cents for each twenty-five pounds exported . . ."

The money was collected, the chamber of deputies passed the enabling act, and construction began. There were no Costa Rican builders with experience in such construction, so fifty foremen from Italy were brought in to teach the local workers. The Costa Ricans learned so quickly that soon they were turning out beautiful stone, wood, and metalwork. The Costa Rican ambassador in Paris scoured Europe for both sculpture and works of art to fill the building as well as for the finest European artists to work on it.

The resulting structure, the National Theater, has for decades been the pride of all Costa Rica and has been ranked as one of the two finest opera houses in the western hemisphere. It is smaller, but perhaps no less magnificent, than the huge opera house of Buenos Aires, Argentina.

The walls were covered with beautiful paintings by famous Italian artists, and most of the ceilings were adorned with striking works of art. Many of the scenes shown represent areas of the country. The finest marbles and other materials were imported for use in this structure.

Grand as the building is, however, the National Theater has a far deeper meaning to the people of Costa Rica than just an architecturally beautiful structure. To them it has become a symbol of the culture of the nation and its continuous spirit of self-improvement.

The magnificent interior of the National Theater (opposite) has been decorated with majestic marble columns, beautifully designed furniture, gleaming parquet floors, and gold laminated ornaments. Even the ceiling is covered with beautiful mural paintings representing Dawn, Day, and Night.

**PAN AMERICAN UNION**

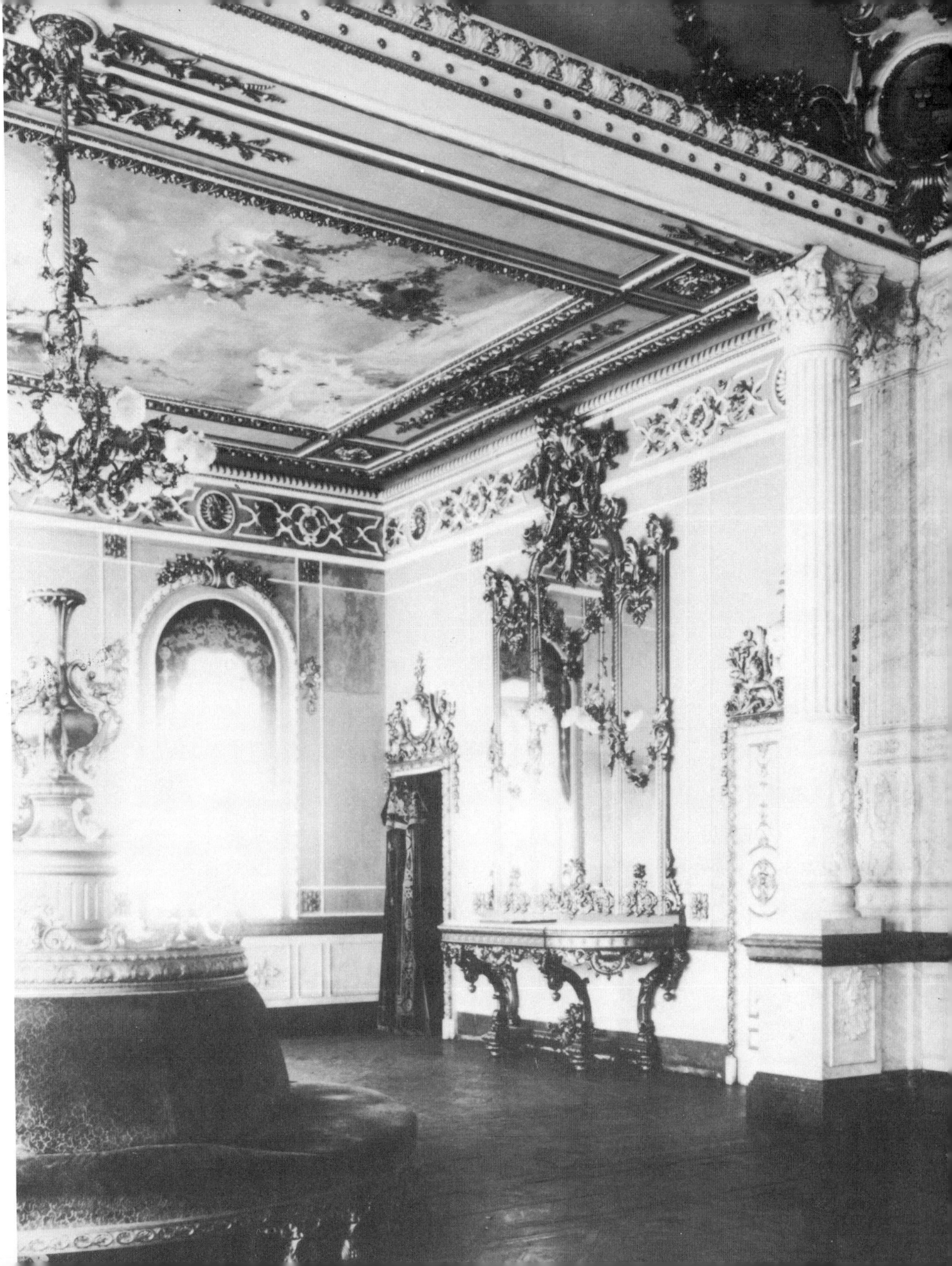

# The Face of the Land

**VOLCANIC SALUTE**

In most countries, visiting presidents are welcomed with a twenty-one-gun salute, but the people of Costa Rica like to say that they salute presidents with volcanic eruptions. This legend began in 1963 when President John F. Kennedy

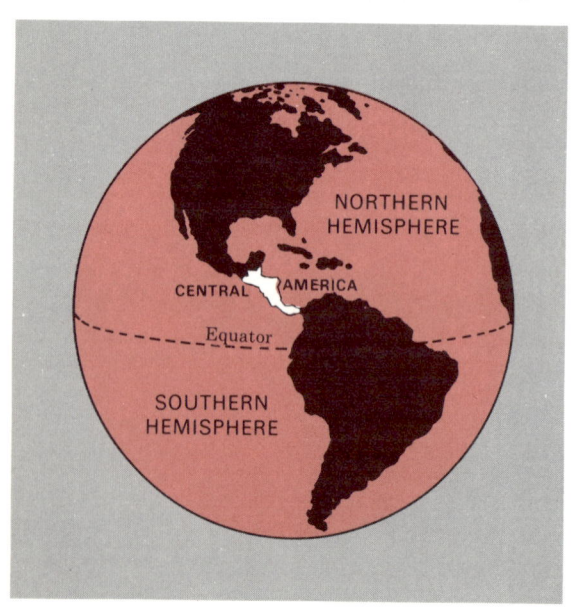

The summit of smoking Irazú volcano may be reached by any traveler who cares to make the 1 ½ hour journey from San José.

PAN AMERICAN UNION

visited the country, and famed volcano Irazú erupted. The legend seemed to be confirmed when the volcano Arenal erupted for the 1968 visit of President Lyndon B. Johnson.

Costa Rica has enough volcanoes to have one ready no matter how many presidents come, although most of the many volcanoes of the country are no longer very active.

The three principal mountain ranges of Costa Rica are mainly volcanic. They run from northwest to southeast and generally parallel the Pacific shoreline, lying much nearer the Pacific than the Caribbean. The most northerly mountain group is known as the Guanacaste Range, the middle range is naturally known as Cordillera Central, while the southwestern range is the Talamanca.

There are smaller local ranges and clusters of hills. The comparatively small Nicoya Peninsula has mountains which rise as high as 3,000 feet, soaring almost directly out of the Pacific Ocean and the Gulf of Nicoya.

The highest mountains of the country are in the Talamanca Range. Here is the loftiest point in Costa Rica—Mount Chirripó Grande—at 12,530 feet. In this range the Pan American Highway crosses the continental divide and reaches its greatest elevation in Central America.

Although a few of the volcanoes are still active, they have not been very violent in recent years. Irazú and Poás smoke most of the time, and occasionally disturb the peaceful Costa Rican countryside with mild eruptions. They are among the few active volcanoes in the world that can be seen at very close range by any visitor who cares to make the trip. The remote, lofty, and rather eerie summits of both volcanoes can be reached in a one and a half hour automobile drive from San José. The mammoth mouth of Poás volcano is said by many authorities to be the largest volcanic crater in the world.

Another volcano of interest to visitors is Turrialba, which takes its name from the white crown of snow on its summit. Its peak cannot be reached by road, but visitors are intrigued by the deep, low rumblings heard occasionally, evidence that the great peak may be only slumbering.

Aside from the interest to tourists, the volcanoes have made other contributions to Costa Rica. Perhaps most important is the deep and fertile coating of volcanic ash which makes the finest type of soil for growing coffee.

### FEATURES OF THE FACE

On the map, Costa Rica appears to have a very unusual shape with two very large "hooks" jutting out of the Pacific coastline of the country. These two oddly formed peninsulas, Nicoya and Osa, by some strange coincidence have almost identical shapes. A part of the peninsula that ends at Point Burica is also within Costa Rican territory; the other part of this peninsula is in Panama.

Because of peninsulas, bays, and other shoreline irregularities, the Pacific Coast is almost five times longer than the Caribbean. The Caribbean shore extends for 133 miles; the Pacific, if stretched out straight, would extend for about 635 miles.

The Gulf of Nicoya alone reaches inland for forty miles. In that gulf are a number of islands; the largest island, Chira, has two small villages. The famed treasure island of Cocos, some distance out in the Pacific, also belongs to Costa Rica.

Costa Rica is about the size of West Virginia in the United States, covering less than 20,000 square miles. Except for Panama, it occupies the narrowest part of the Central American isthmus. The distance across, from sea to sea, varies between the widest point of 174 miles and the narrowest, about 75 miles.

The country is divided into three very distinct land types. Along both coasts lie the lowlands, sometimes swampy, some-

### MAP KEY

Alajuela D3
Atlanta D6
Cañas R. D2
Caño Is. F4
Cartago D4
Cape Blanco E2
Cape Matapalo G5
Cape St. Elena C1
Cape Velas D1
Chira Island D2
Chirripó R. C4
Cordillera Central D4
Coronado Bay F4
Corredor F6
Diquis R. F5
Dulce Gulf F5
Golfito F5
Grande R. D3
Guacimo D5
Gulf of Nicoya E3
Heredia D3
Irazú Vol. D4
Laguna de Arenal C2
Liberia C2
Limón D6
Mt. Chirripó Grande E5
Nicoya D2
Orosi D4
Palmar Sur F5
Papagayo Gulf C1
Paraiso D4
Parrita E3
Península de Nicoya D2
Península de Osa F5
Piedras Blancas F5
Poás Vol. D3
Point Burica G6
Point Cahuita D6
Point Guiones D1
Puerto Cortés F4
Puntarenas D2
Quepos E4
Reventazón R. D5
San Isidro E4
San José D3
San Juan R. C4
San Ramón D3
Sarapiquí R. C4
Santa Cruz D1
Sierra de Tilarán D3
Sixaola D6
Sixaola R. D6
Tempisque R. D1
Turrialba Vol. D4

A
B
C
D
E
5
6
Lake Nicaragua
NICARAGUA
CARIBBEAN
SEA
PACIFIC OCEAN
Cape St. Elena
Papagayo Gulf
Cape Velas
Point Guiones
Cape Blanco
Gulf of Nicoya
CORDILLERA DE GUANACASTE
LIBERIA
Lake Arenal
SIERRA DE TILARÁN
CORDILLERA CENTRAL
Tempisque R.
Cañas R.
Santa Cruz
Nicoya
Chira Island
PENÍNSULA DE NICOYA
PUNTARENAS
Grande R.
SAN JOSÉ
SAN RAMÓN
ALAJUELA
HEREDIA
POÁS VOL.
IRAZÚ VOL.
TURRIALBA VOL.
CARTAGO
PARAISO
OROSI
TURRIALBA
GUACIMO
San Juan R.
Sarapiquí R.
Chirripó R.
Reventazón R.
LIMÓN
ATLANTA
Point Cahuita
Sixaola R.
CORDILLERA DE TALAMANCA
MT. CHIRRIPÓ GRANDE
PARRITA
QUEPOS
SAN ISIDRO
Diquís R.
PUERTOS CORTÉS
PALMAR SUR
Coronado Bay
Caño Island
PIEDRAS BLANCAS
GOLFITO
CORREDOR
PENÍNSULA DE OSA
Dulce Gulf
Cape Matapalo
Point Burica
PANAMA

times grassy, frequently forested. Higher, at altitudes of 3,000 to 6,500 feet, lies the temperate zone of the country. Above 6,500 feet stand the mountain regions.

Most important of all is the great Central Valley, in the temperate zone, ranging from 3,000 to 6,000 feet in altitude. In this area of only about 2,000 square miles lives 75 percent of the entire population of the country. The Central Valley is almost entirely surrounded by the Talamanca Mountains to the south and the Central Range to the north.

### DRAINING THE LAND

There are no major lakes in Costa Rica. Of the small ones to be found in the country, the largest are Arenal and Cóter.

However, for a country its size, Costa Rica has many rivers. Thirty-four river basins are described in the Costa Rica book of the *Regional Analysis of Physical Resources* series.

In the north, several rivers begin in Costa Rica and flow into huge Lake Nicaragua in Nicaragua. Some of these rivers are Frio, Sapoa, Mena, Haciendas, Cucaracha, Pizote, Guacalito, Zapote, and the Chilito.

The largest river to touch Costa Rica is the San Juan, main outlet of mammoth Lake Nicaragua. A number of rivers have their beginning in the Costa Rican highlands south of the San Juan and flow north to join it. The most important of these are the San Carlos and the Sarapiquí. The San Juan has an unusual mouth which splits into a number of rivers to form its delta. Two of these split-off rivers have been named the Caño Bravo and the Colorado. Later, the Caño Bravo and the Colorado again come together; then the Colorado splits into one of the strangest river mouths anywhere. Just before it reaches the sea an island blocks the river's passage. It swings away to the north around the island into an odd H-shaped formation. It also flows south and then north again to form another island which fronts on the Caribbean.

Other rivers emptying into the Caribbean are the Tortuguero, Parismina, Pacuare, Reventazón, Madre de Dios, Matina, Blanco, Limón, Banano, Bananito, and Sixaola; the Palacios and the Chiquero, which are linked by a natural canal, also empty into the Caribbean. The Palacios and Tortuguero flow into the same bay, and the Pacuare and Madre de Dios share another bay. For a considerable part of its length, the Sixaola is the boundary river with Panama.

Several small rivers cut through the northwest shores to the Pacific. The main river of the northwest is the Tempisque, emptying into the Gulf of Nicoya. A number of other small rivers flow down the western slopes to the Pacific, continuing on to the Nicoya Peninsula. Among the larger of these are the Rio Grande de Térraba, emptying into Coronado Bay, the Rio Pirris, and Rio Grande de Tárcoles.

## IN ANCIENT TIMES

Geologists divide Costa Rica into three different sections: the Outer Arch, the Inner Arch, and the Limón Basin. It is thought that the Outer Arch, what is now the Pacific Coast, was once a chain of volcanic islands. Over vast ages of time, lava from volcanoes built up the land and welded the islands together. As ages passed, the land was worn down and smoothed by the action of wind and water.

The central mountains (Inner Arch) are much more recent. They were formed partly by the uplifting of the earth's crust but mostly by the almost constant flow of volcanic lava over eons of time. They remain higher today because erosion has not yet washed away the soil.

The Limón Basin was formed by a slow rising of the land level. Rivers and rains from the higher lands to the west deposited sediment to form the rather flat lands of the Caribbean Coast.

## CLIMATE

Lowland Costa Rica is just plain hot, with temperatures frequently in the nineties. The entire coast and land well into Alajuela Department is classed as "tropical wet" climate. There may be as many as three hundred days of rain each year.

In spite of this lowland heat and humidity, for most Costa Ricans the weather is springlike—warm during the day and cooler at night. The Central Valley and other higher areas where the bulk of the population lives are cooled by their elevation and the people really do live in "eternal spring." Even in the Central Valley, however, there are considerable climate differences depending on location. The climate of Cartago, for instance, is not as comfortable as that of San José just a few miles away, for Cartago is swept by many of the great eastern rains, while San José is sheltered from them by the mountains.

San José has a generally delightful climate, never changing very much from month to month. There are warm days and cool nights which give the capital and its general area the same kind of perpetual spring weather shared with most of the other capitals of Central America.

The whole Caribbean Coast and most of the northern region have a climate known as "tropical wet." The whole southern Pacific Coast and part of the Pacific portion of the Nicoya Peninsula is also in the tropical wet zone. The northwest climate ranges from tropical wet to dry. Most of the rest of the country's climate is classed as "warm temperate."

# Four Boys and Girls of Costa Rica

### SEBASTIAN OF SAN JOSÉ

Sebastian was trembling with excitement as he broke open the mold. "Very good," his father exclaimed as he first saw the glittering object. "It looks much like the original. Your mother will be surprised and very pleased."

Sebastian is a Josefino (resident of San José) who lives with his family in the capital city of Costa Rica. He has been interested for a long time in the works of the prehistoric people of his country, especially their beautifully fashioned objects of pure gold. Some time ago, Sebastian's father had given him a hobby kit for casting metal by what is known as the "lost wax" process. He had previously used this kit to cast some reproductions of prehistoric jewelry, using inexpensive metals such as lead.

As a surprise for his mother's birthday, however, Sebastian was allowed to reproduce in gold a simple but beautiful

Sebastian is fascinated by these golden amulets made by prehistoric Costa Rican Indians, who designed beautifully fashioned objects of pure gold.

COLLECTION FROM
THE NATIONAL MUSEUM
OF COSTA RICA
PAN AMERICAN UNION

prehistoric Indian pendant in the form of an owl. The original solid gold pendant is shown in the National Museum of San José. Since Sebastian's father knows most of the people at the museum, Sebastian was permitted to take a wax impression from which he made his reproduction.

Sebastian's father, a banker, is one of the very wealthy men of San José, and he is anxious to provide his son opportunities to pursue almost any subject that interests him. In turn, Sebastian takes an interest in almost everything about his city and his beloved country.

The father's business interests keep him traveling much of the time, and he takes Sebastian with him as often as possible. They have traveled both north and south on the Pan American Highway. Sebastian will never forget the trip to Panama City in the family limousine. They were not quite sure the big Mercedes Benz was going to make it around some of the curves, and they thought they might bounce right through the roof.

In spite of the curves and some rough spots in the road, however, Sebastian and his father especially enjoyed the stretch of highway along the crest of the Talamanca Range. Here the road runs along the continental divide at its highest point in all of Central America. Finally they reached Panama City, which Sebastian did not like very well because it seemed so very hot after the wonderful cool weather of San José. However, Sebastian greatly enjoyed watching the operation of the locks of the Panama Canal.

The drive the family took north on the Pan American Highway through Nicaragua past great Lake Nicaragua, through Honduras and El Salvador to Guatemala City was much easier. There weren't so many curves and the roads were much better most of the way. Sebastian particularly enjoyed the visits they made to several Indian villages, especially Chichicastenango in Guatemala. He is sorry that there are only a few Indians left in his own country.

Generally when Sebastian's family goes to the port city of Limón, they fly or go by car, but once they took the train from San José. Sebastian had never been on a steam train before, and he hung halfway out the window most of the trip, watching the colorful trees and flowers, the friendly people at the stations, the coffee and banana plantations along the way, and especially the people who live in the region of Limón.

Sebastian likes the quick trip by electric railroad or the leisurely drive in the car to the Pacific Ocean port of Puntarenas. He loves to fish, swim, and water ski in the warm clear waters of the ocean there.

Fine El Coco airport is only a few minutes' drive over a superhighway from the family's big four-level modern home in San José. Sebastian has flown with his father on business to New York City and Los Angeles, and the family has vacationed in Paris, London, and Madrid.

Sebastian attends one of the excellent private schools of San José. He loyally plans to enroll at the fine University of Costa Rica in a suburb of San José, but he expects to finish his business courses in one of the great universities of Europe or the United States before he joins his father's many enterprises.

Sebastian loves the sights and activities of his native city more than those he has seen on his trips abroad. Particularly impressive to him are the services that the family attends regularly in the Cathedral of San José. Every Sunday morning they thrill to the music of the fine choir, and Sebastian loves to see the men of the military band in full uniform, sitting straight and proud in the pews.

He goes with his family to the Country Club or the Tennis Club where society of San José gathers. He also roots enthusiastically along with everyone else in the capital when the local soccer team plays in the stadium just outside the capital city.

Because of his father's position, Sebastian has an inside view of many important events. He was impressed with the welcome that San José gave to the United States President Lyndon Johnson in 1968. Sebastian was rather surprised when his father laughingly said Costa Rica had to borrow a cannon from Panama to give Mr. Johnson a twenty-one-gun salute, since they had no artillery of their own. He knows that his country is perhaps the only one in the world with no national army.

The family was in the official party during the ceremonies in which José Figueres Ferrer took office as President of Costa Rica in early 1970. Sebastian admires President Figueres and wishes the people would not call him *El Enano* (The Dwarf), just because he is not very tall.

Sebastian wonders if some day he might be president of his country. He has a good start toward the realization of such an ambition.

### JUAN OF LIBERIA

Although Juan's family is as wealthy as Sebastian's, Juan leads an entirely different kind of life. He lives in a great rambling *hacienda*, or farm house, on a ranch of thousands of acres which has been controlled by his family for many generations.

The closest town to the family's main estate is the small city of Liberia, capital of Guanacaste Province. The great ranch, however, is almost entirely self-contained. Nearly all the food needed is grown there, and the women of the ranch do much of the necessary weaving and sewing as well as cooking. Juan's father, who is known as the *patrón*, provides schools and teachers for the children of the ranch. These teachers give private tutoring to Juan and his younger brothers and sisters.

Life on the ranch is much like that on the great ranches in some of the other countries of Central and South America. However, families of great wealth who own large ranches are not very common in Costa Rica. Most of the few really large estates of Costa Rica are found in Juan's part of the country. They are owned by

Juan's father, the *patrón* of a huge ranch, provides schools and teachers for the children of the men and women who work and live on the ranch. Below, children of plantation workers on a ranch much like that of Juan's father play soccer on a playground the rancher has provided for them.

UNITED FRUIT COMPANY

the pure-blooded descendants of the Spanish aristocrats who settled there in early times.

The life of Guanacaste Province is a free and open one, spent as much as possible in the beautiful wide countryside. Guanacaste is noted for its capable cowboys who ride the cattle herds of the leading estancias. Juan himself has been riding since he was very young and is almost as good a horseman as his father and the other men of the great ranch. He is proud of his own horse and is now entirely responsible for his care.

Juan "dresses" his horse according to the local custom. He has a fine saddle, but hopes some day to have one as good as the beautiful saddle his father uses. Every cowboy Juan knows has spent more than he should have on his saddle, and each one still yearns to have a more beautiful one for his own horse.

Under the saddle, Juan places a kind of skirtlike blanket made of fleece. He fastens bright artificial flowers and bows to the horse's mane and colorful tassels and rosettes on his cruppers.

Juan enjoys everything about outdoor life. He loves to go with his father on hunting trips into the foothills of the Guanacaste Cordillera. His father once shot an ocelot, and Juan was lucky enough to get a wild pig. They have both bagged deer, fox, and rabbit.

Juan also loves to fish. The rivers and streams near his home abound with many kinds of fish, but he particularly likes deep-sea fishing. His father has a wealthy friend who has a spread near the tiny Pacific Coast village of Playas del Coco. Juan and his father drive over the road from Liberia to Playas del Coco. The road is not very good over the final stretch, but they both think the fishing is worth the discomfort, especially when at last they cast their lines from the friend's private fishing boat and feel the tug of an important catch.

Several times Juan has caught snook, but his greatest thrill came when he had a good-sized sailfish on the line; he was disappointed when it got away. He was almost frightened one time when his father caught a large manta ray, a batlike fish.

Juan enjoys the pleasant times when his family entertains at the estancia. The people of Guanacaste Province are extremely hospitable and love to entertain their neighbors and friends. Even strangers are entertained as close friends. Since there are few hotels in the area, most visitors are entertained in private homes.

In this "wild west" of Costa Rica, it is not surprising that the principal entertainment is the *asada,* an outdoor barbecue feast. When great sides of meat are hung on racks above large fires of blazing coals and cooked in the open, the delicious aroma of the browning meat fills the air.

Almost everyone in the area attends the asada, and the people of the ranch love to provide entertainment. The national dance, the *punto guanacasteco*, originated in the region and Juan thinks his father's helpers dance the guanacasteco better than anyone at other asadas he has attended.

He loves to watch them stamping and whirling to the rhythms of the marimba and guitar. Many other songs and dances began in the region and spread to wider popularity.

Once in awhile one of the older men plays the Indian ocarina, or the ancient *chirimía* (like an oboe), while someone else taps out the beat on a native drum known as the *quijongo*.

Juan also loves the many fiestas of the region. Generally these end in the nearest town square with the young fellows of the region trying to outdo one another in a kind of primitive bullfight. These contests generally draw to a close without much damage to either bull or bullfighters. Juan has never taken part in any of these, but he would dearly like to try when he gets a little older. He is sure his father won't mind, although his mother probably will.

In addition to the main ranch, Juan's father owns one of the famous orchid farms near Paraiso and one of the equally famous farms near Coris, where pure-bred Arabian horses are raised. Juan has driven with his father to these places, and so he has been to San José and Cartago, as well as to Puntarenas, nearer his home.

Juan does not care much for the cities, however. He cannot imagine living anywhere but on the family's great estate, where he will take over some day as the *patrón*.

Nevertheless, Juan knows that times are changing, and even the holders of big estates must keep up with the times, so he is already planning to take his university work at Cornell University in New York State in the United States. There he will study the management of large agricultural holdings, as well as the very fine liberal education courses that a young man of his position feels he must have. With this fine education and his many experiences, it is probable that Juan will become one of the real leaders of his country.

## NEGRITA OF CARTAGO

It was the largest cart she had ever painted, and Negrita stood off to admire her work. Really, it did look very much like the carts she had seen so often on the country roads near her home in Cartago. She felt quite proud of her work.

Negrita lives with her parents in a rather modest home in one of the newer sections of the ancient city of Cartago. Her father is one of the health inspectors for the public health department of Cartago. According to the country's constitution, every city and town of the country must spend at least 20 percent of its total income to promote the health of its people. Thus, cities such as Cartago have much more advanced public health services than would be expected for communities of their size in Latin America. In the Cartago division of the health department there are 315 employees, including 30 doctors, 14 nurses, and 91 nurse's aides.

Negrita's father enjoys his hobby of woodworking, and he has a small shop with a number of woodworking tools. Not

Negrita has been learning the art of painting oxcarts, for which her country is well known. Here a man paints the wheel of a cart that will be entered in competition. He hopes to win an award for the most beautifully decorated cart.

PAN AMERICAN UNION

long ago he made a small model of one of the famous oxcarts of Costa Rica. Traditionally these are decorated with wonderful original designs in the brightest of colors. Negrita has always been good at painting, and she volunteered to paint the first small cart that her father made. When the owner of a craft shop in San José happened to see the model cart, he insisted on buying it to sell in his shop.

The craft shop owner normally carries reproductions of carts manufactured in factories in Costa Rica. However, he says that the factory-made carts look too polished to be good imitations of the cruder, handmade, hand-decorated carts actually used on the farms. He thought the cart Negrita and her father made was much more natural looking. He sold their model right away and will buy all they can make as soon as they have them ready. The large one they have just finished is to be taken apart and shipped to the United States where the man who bought it plans to use it as a counter from which to serve drinks in his recreation room. Most people

The cart in the picture above is completed and ready for competition. Negrita enjoys her painting hobby but isn't sure she could ever paint an oxcart that would be beautiful enough to win an award. For now she will paint only models.

PAN AMERICAN UNION

prefer to buy the more realistic-looking carts, but there are few to be found.

This hobby, which she very much enjoys, enables Negrita to put away regularly a nice sum of money to be used for her future education. At present she attends elementary school. She is now in sixth grade. Next year she will start secondary school and when she has finished her five-year course, she must take a very complete examination. When she passes this, she will proudly possess the title of Bachelor of Science and Letters. These school years correspond to high school as well as the early part of a college course in the United States. Negrita hopes to attend the University of Costa Rica and become a pharmacist. However, she is also interested in the possibility of studying nursing; there is a real need for nurses in her country, as elsewhere.

Because the capital is only about fifteen miles from Cartago by a good two-lane highway, Negrita has visited San José many times, going in the old but sturdy family car. The family says that her father

Negrita enjoys the feast day of August 2 when the tiny black stone statue called La Negrita is honored. The statue is kept in an altar in the Shrine of Our Lady of the Angels (left) in Negrita's town, Cartago.

**G. KHACHADOURIAN**

cares for the car as tenderly as he watches out for the health of the people. Because the price of cars is so high, this one will have to serve them all for a long time.

Negrita has several favorite places she likes to visit in San José. She likes to attend the military band concerts in the fine band shell of Central Park, but most of all she is fascinated by the great National Theater. She loves art and thinks the fine murals and decorations on the theater's walls are the most wonderful things she has ever seen. Negrita also likes to visit the National Museum where she especially enjoys the pottery, gold work, and other art pieces that were made by the Indians of Costa Rica hundreds of years ago. She marvels at the skill those people had at such an early time.

Negrita has gone to the central market on Avenida Central in San José, but she thinks the market in her home town is much superior, especially the market held every Sunday. She loves to watch the colorful crowds, and she is very proud that the many craftsmen of her country can create such fine work in wood, leather, ceramics, and metal. Negrita might someday try to sell some of her pictures there.

The family's favorite excursion is up the twisting road that leads to the very top of Mt. Irazú, at the base of which Cartago itself nestles. They enjoy the lovely drive, leading upward over a crazy, crooked road. When the family car finally pants up to the parking lot at the top, everyone is almost quivering with excitement. They hurry down the path of hardened volcanic ash, up the side of the crater itself, and finally stand on the brink of what sometimes is a boiling cauldron of red-hot lava. If they are lucky, it will be a day on which Irazú stirs slightly in its slumbers and puffs out much smoke and steam. On a clear day they can admire the wonderful views of both the Pacific and Atlantic oceans.

Negrita was only a tiny girl in 1963 when Mt. Irazú had its strongest eruption in modern history, and all of Cartago was overshadowed by an awesome cloud of ash and smoke. She can still remember the fear she felt at the time and wonders what they would do if such a terrible thing were to happen while they stand there.

Even more than the trip up Irazú, however, Negrita enjoys the feast day of August 2. This is the day when most of Central America honors the tiny black stone statue called La Negrita, from which Negrita was given her name, although she has no black ancestors.

The statue is kept permanently in a beautiful, decorated altar in the Shrine of Our Lady of the Angels in Cartago. Every year on the feast day of the Virgin, thousands of people gather on the streets of Cartago to watch the little figurine as it is taken in solemn but joyous procession down the city streets to another church and then is brought back to the shrine to rest there for another year. Each year Negrita watches this procession proudly and vows that when she grows up she will live up to her name by having a career of service to her people.

## MINOR OF LIMÓN

This was surely the happiest day of his life, Minor thought. When his father had come home, he had hugged him and kissed him and hung on as if he never would let him go again. It seemed a long time ago that Minor's father had become ill and the doctor thought he had tuberculosis. He had gone to the wonderful sanitorium of Duran, nestled on the slopes of the volcano Irazú. Minor knew that this was a fine place; the local doctor said it was one of the best of its kind in all of Latin America. Happily, the lung illness was not tuberculosis, so after considerable treatment his father was back home and the doctor said he would be completely well again.

Minor's father works as a dock supervisor for the great fruit company which operates much of the business of the Limón region where the family lives; company operations include a large part of the port, railroads, and other activities of the community. Minor and his family live in one of the comfortable houses provided by the company; the health care given his father was also made available through the company's program.

Minor and his parents are Negroes, as are a majority of the residents of the Limón area. Minor's great-great grandfather came to Costa Rica from the island of Jamaica to help with the building of the important railroad which connected Limón with San José, the capital. The unusual American who was most responsible for the successful completion of the railroad was Minor Cooper Keith. Our Minor's great-great grandfather was so impressed with Mr. Keith's accomplishments that he named his first son Minor in honor of the railroad builder. Since that time there has always been at least one Minor in the family, and our Minor is the latest namesake in that tradition. He is very proud of his name and hopes to do something important to honor his namesake.

In fact, Minor has a rather unusual ambition. Almost as long as he can remember he has wanted to be a writer. He has already had a poem published in one of the local newspapers; he wrote it in both English and Spanish. English is the language of his home, but all children of the area learn Spanish as the official language of their country. Minor attends a new and very well-equipped school in Limón which is operated by the government. Because he is such a brilliant boy, he has no fear of his coming examination for the Bachelor of Science and Letters.

Minor's future education seems to be assured. The fruit company has taken an interest in him ever since he began to lead his class in his studies. They will probably offer him an advanced education if he plans to return and work for them. They would perhaps want him to attend the Inter-American Institute of Agricultural Science at Turrialba and prepare to be a banana scientist. However, they do not know about his ambition to be a writer, and he may not be interested in working

Minor and his family live in a comfortable home provided by the fruit company for which Minor's father works. The banana plantation homes in the picture above are similar to the one in which Minor lives.

UNITED FRUIT COMPANY

for the company. In that case, it is likely that there will be a scholarship for him at the University of Costa Rica near San José or even at a university in the United States under one of the international scholarship plans.

Minor has already decided on the type of writing he wants to do. He is fascinated by the work of many Costa Rican writers, especially Argüello Mora and the priest who was also a prose writer and a poet, Father Juan Garita. These men and others write in a very natural and informal style about the details of the life of everyday people. In Costa Rica this writing style has a picturesque name—*Costumbrismo*.

Someday Minor hopes he will be able to write in the Costumbrismo style. He observes the people around him carefully, and takes notes on what he sees and the thoughts that come to him. He is especially anxious to travel, although he has not been able to do much of that. The only long trip he has taken was when he went alone on the train to visit his uncle in San José. His uncle, who is not many years older than Minor, works as a ticket salesman in one of the airline offices there.

On the train trip, both ways, Minor scarcely took his head out of the window except to watch the butcher boys pass up and down the aisles of the cars selling their wares. He could scarcely believe a city could be as big or as busy and crowded as San José. He and his uncle went to almost every place of importance in the city, and Minor's notebook is bulging with the detailed notes he took. He already has written several short sketches about the trip.

## FOUR FOR ALL AND ALL FOR FOUR

Sebastian, Juan, Negrita, and Minor are all very different in their experiences and outlooks on life. They have lived so differently that they seem worlds apart in many ways, but they are all loyal Costa Ricans, and it is likely that when they grow up they will all find many different ways to serve their beloved country and make it a better place for their children and for those who come after them.

# Costa Rica Yesterday

### ANCIENT COSTA RICANS

Little is known about the people who inhabited Costa Rica tens of centuries ago. However, it is generally agreed that people must have occupied the land for thousands of years, although no ruins of great cities like those of the Mayan people farther to the north have been found.

There must have been a well-developed civilization in the area at one time, however. In Merced Park, San José, visitors can see a huge rock that was carved into the rough shape of a globe by some unknown people of the area. This is only one of the several mementos left behind by a race that has been completely forgotten except for those relics.

Even better evidence of pre-European civilization has been found, although of more recent date. By the time the first explorers from Europe found them, the native people were doing skilled work in stone carving, weaving, and especially fine metalwork, indicating that these skills must have been carried on for generations.

The prehistoric peoples of Costa Rica must be ranked among the world's finest early goldsmiths. Many museums have truly amazing exhibits of the gold work done by them.

One of the most striking pieces of prehistoric art still in existence is a Costa Rican pendant made in the shape of an alligator god, now owned by the Museum of Primitive Art in New York. It is very large for a piece of solid gold, and the head is attached to the body with a movable hinge very unusual for its time. There are inlays of pyrite in the abdomen and

The golden Indian amulets pictured here were fashioned by prehistoric peoples of Costa Rica, who were among the finest gold workers in the ancient Americas.

**COLLECTION FROM THE
NATIONAL MUSEUM OF COSTA RICA
PAN AMERICAN UNION**

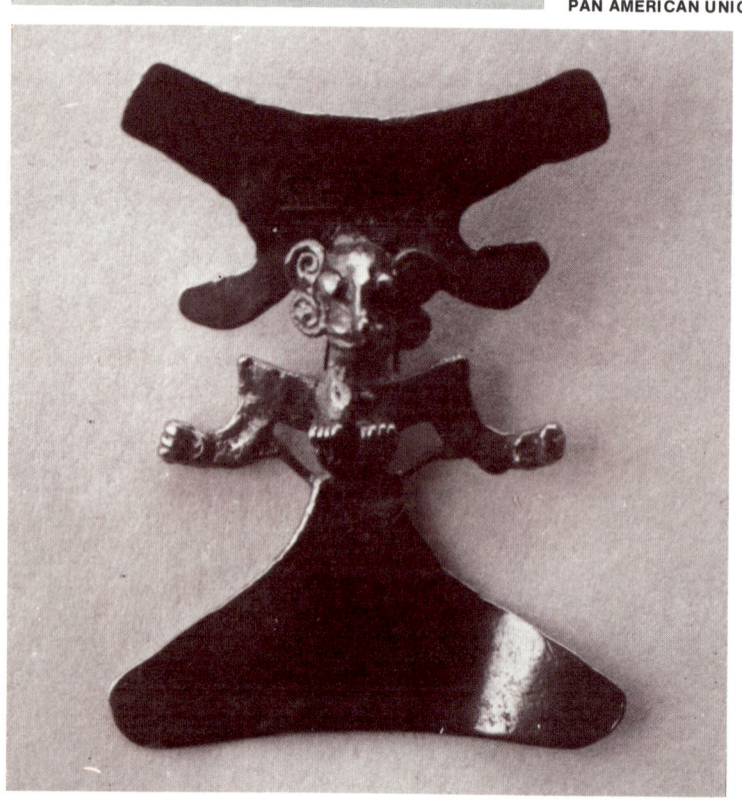

eyes. The sides of the head are decorated with other alligator figures in gold and similar figures are carved on both sides of the nose. The piece is beautifully done and must have been created by a skilled artist.

The early gold artists cast many animal figures in gold—owls and other birds, armadillos, as well as alligators. These ancient gold workers cast their figures by a process known as the lost-wax method. Even today lost wax pieces require highly skilled workmanship.

One of the most interesting gold figures, still preserved by William Jaffe of New York City, is the gold figure of a man, found in the region known as Linea Vieja. The figure, with eyes closed to slits, is beautifully cast and has a very realistic appearance. The right hand holds some kind of staff or weapon, topped by three round objects.

Although Panama and Colombia are said to have had the finest gold workers among the ancient peoples of America, in some ways the gold objects found in Costa Rica are fully as good, sometimes even better.

The Chorotega tribe was renowned for its work in carving jade. This work is thought to have been influenced by the Mayan civilization. In the opinion of some experts, however, the ruins left by the Chorotegas in Guanacaste Province are linked to the Aztec culture.

The Chorotegas also were noted for their striking pottery. Among the noteworthy examples of this work is a large pottery jar, which rests on three chunky legs. Across the surface of this jar is a fearsome crawling lizard, in raised and painted design. His head is lifted angrily from the surface of the jar, and he scowls ferociously.

The Boruca people, in what is now southwestern Costa Rica, were especially skilled in making brown-colored textiles. The weaving was done in such a way that the design appeared on only one side of the cloth. Many natives of Costa Rica are reviving this craft in modern times.

Before the Europeans came, the native peoples were mostly agricultural, growing corn, beans, cotton, and yucca. They were few in numbers, probably not more than twenty-five thousand altogether, and were scattered over the entire area; most lived in the Central Valley.

## A RICH COAST?

Christopher Columbus was sailing off the Caribbean Coast of Central America on his fourth voyage, the last he made to the New World. Suddenly, on September 18, 1502, a fierce storm drove the explorer to seek shelter. He landed at a very old Indian village called Cariari (now Limón) and became the first known European to find what is now Costa Rica. Columbus went on a modest exploring expedition and found that the area was inhabited by three major Indian tribes: the Boruca, Chorotega, and Güetare. Each of these major tribes was governed by a chief known as a cacique.

Only twenty years later, in 1522, Spanish exploration had reached the Pacific Coast, as Spanish adventurers explored the Nicoya Peninsula. Expecting to find much gold in the region, the Spanish named it Costa Rica, which means Rich Coast. They were disappointed, however, for no enormous riches were ever discovered there.

As a result of the west coast exploration, the first Spanish settlement in Costa Rica came into being; established near the present city of Puntarenas, it was known as Bruselas. Bruselas lasted only about three years. And the other outpost-type settlements that sprang up were also short-lived.

### THE SPANISH PERIOD

In 1564, Don Juan Vásquez de Coronado founded the first permanent settlement—Cartago. When he became governor—the only peaceful Spanish conquistador (conqueror) in the New World—Coronado started a program to take over Costa Rica. This unusual Spanish nobleman understood that the rich and pleasant Central Valley could make a fine home for settlers. He persuaded fifty families from Aragón and Galicia provinces in Spain to settle there. In addition, Coronado brought horses, cattle, and swine to the new settlement. It is thought that the cattle ranch Coronado established may have been the first of its kind in the entire western hemisphere.

Coronado's untimely death at sea during a voyage to Spain brought an end to one of the most peaceful rules in all of Spanish America.

After his death, Costa Rica became one of the seven "gobernaciones" of Central America—all governed from Guatemala by a "Capitanía General" and a high court of justice known as a "Real Audiencia." The local Spanish governor, whose capital was at Cartago, held office for a five-year term. His authority included political, judicial, and military rule.

During all the Spanish period, Costa Rica enjoyed a kind of peace and tranquility that was scarcely known elsewhere in the entire Spanish world. Because the country was isolated from much of the other Spanish territory, and had no great treasures, it escaped the turmoil that made life so bitter in much of the Spanish area.

However, the peaceful land did not escape one great hazard. Over a period of nearly three hundred years, English and Dutch pirate raiders terrorized the countryside. One of the most famous of these pirate attacks occurred in 1666. The British pirates Morgan and Mansfield drew their ships up to Portete on the Caribbean and decided to loot and despoil the whole country.

Governor Juan López de la Flor could gather only a handful of fighting men to defend the country. Those who could not

---

Opposite: The Bainbridge portrait of Christopher Columbus, the first known European to discover what is now Costa Rica.

**PAN AMERICAN UNION**

CHRISTOBAL COLON

fight hurried to the mission of Ujarrás to pray. The much weaker defenders beat off a fierce pirate force about seven hundred strong. The prayers of those who had gathered in the church were credited with the victory.

Heredia was founded in 1717, and San José did not come into existence until 1737. Progress was far from rapid. By 1751 in the entire Central Valley there were fewer than twenty-five hundred people, members of only four hundred different families. Costa Rica might have grown more quickly if Spain had not regulated the trade of her colonies. Costa Rica was not permitted to trade with any nation except Spain, and Spanish trade was divided among the entire hemisphere.

### END OF SPANISH RULE

These stifling trade rules were one of the main reasons why lands all across the hemisphere under Spanish rule began to insist on independence. The provinces of Central America were particularly fortunate in this conflict. They had never had as much value to Spain as had Mexico, Peru, and other rich lands of the Americas. When revolt and discontent swept many of the countries at about the same time, Spain was busy dealing with revolutions from one end of Latin America to the other. Because the Spanish armies could not be spread so thin, there was almost no Spanish armed might in Central America.

A group of Central American leaders meeting in Guatemala City on September 15, 1821, proclaimed the independence of Central America; there was no armed opposition from Spain. In this most peaceful of all major revolutions, the whole region between Panama and Mexico threw off Spanish rule without bloodshed.

Communication was so slow that more than a month passed before the people of Costa Rica learned of their new freedom. When the news came, the last Spanish governor of Costa Rica resigned his post.

### TIME OF MANY CHANGES

Almost at once, however, the new freedom was threatened. In 1821 the Mexican Empire, ruled by strong man Agustín Iturbide, declared all of Central America to be part of a new and vastly enlarged empire of Mexico. Mexican troops were sent into Guatemala in the first attempt to take over the territory. Within a year, however, this Mexican domain had fallen and with it went most Mexican claims to control of Central America.

With the example of the thirteen states to the north which had managed to establish a United States, the five nations of Central America met in 1823 and agreed to form a Federation of Central America.

This was an eventful year for Costa Rica. During a civil war that year, frequent earthquakes destroyed the capital of Cartago; the capital was moved to nearby San José.

The first of Costa Rica's numerous constitutions was adopted on January 22, 1825, within the framework of the United Provinces of Central America. This union continued for some years, but soon became a union in name only.

### A NEW REPUBLIC

Many factors contributed to the disintegration of the union: The member countries were very different from one another, and had different problems; regular communications between members of the United Provinces were difficult and sometimes impossible to maintain; and the poorly educated people of most Central American countries were not able to support the government of a federation.

The union was kept alive mainly by the devotion and enthusiasm of its leader, Francisco Morazán. However, many leaders in the individual countries were fiercely nationalistic and bitterly opposed to Morazán. Finally, in 1838, the United Provinces of Central America was dissolved and Morazán went into voluntary exile in South America.

When the federation ended in 1838, Costa Rica declared itself an independent nation, and Braulio Carrillo took over the administration. Under his control the government became more orderly and efficient. The economy of the country improved; he did much to encourage coffee growing. Carrillo was particularly effective in teaching the people the impor-

PAN AMERICAN UNION

Almost as soon as the independence of Central America was proclaimed in 1821, the new freedom was threatened by strong man Agustín Iturbide, ruler of the vast Mexican Empire.

tance of work and moral principles in their lives.

In spite of his good points, however, Carrillo ruled as an ironhanded dictator. Members of the Liberal Party, who wanted a more democratic rule, made an appeal to Francisco Morazán to return from South America. He decided to do so and was able to force Carrillo from his leadership in 1842.

Almost as soon as he was made provisional president of Costa Rica in July, Morazán proclaimed that the Central American federation would be reestablished and that Costa Rica would be a member of the union.

To the other Central American countries this seemed to be a declaration of war, and in fact Morazán was preparing for war. He levied heavy taxes to pay for the war effort and became very dictatorial. His popularity quickly declined, and only two months after taking control he was captured by opposition forces. Sentenced to death, Morazán asked his captors if he could command the firing squad himself; the wish was granted and he died in this unusual way.

In 1848, Costa Rica proclaimed itself a republic. In 1850, almost thirty years after the last Spanish governor had been driven out, the independence of the country was finally recognized by Spain.

### THE CASE OF WILLIAM WALKER

Costa Rica was not yet quite free of involvement with the other nations of Cen-

**PAN AMERICAN UNION**
The popularity of Francisco Morazán (above), leader of the United Provinces of Central America, declined when he became dictatorial, and he was executed in 1842.

tral America. The central figure in a very strange episode was an American adventurer named William Walker. This man had lived a varied life as a doctor, a lawyer, and a soldier of fortune. With a ragtag group of followers, Walker had twice invaded Mexico in what were thought to be schemes to form a new country out of Mexican territory.

In 1854 Liberal and Conservative party members in Nicaragua battled for the presidency of that country. When the Conservatives won, the Liberals invited Walker to come to Nicaragua to help them. He assembled a motley group of soldiers of fortune, landed in Nicaragua, and with almost ridiculous ease took control of the country.

Juan Rafael Mora, president of Costa Rica when the country was invaded by William Walker and his filibusters. When President Mora and his forces defeated Walker and the filibusters, Mora became a national hero.

**PAN AMERICAN UNION**

As his power grew in Nicaragua, it became plain that Walker was considering greater conquests. Other countries of Central America feared that he planned to include them in a great Central American Empire under his iron control. The other countries tried to unite to oppose him. Normally peaceful Costa Rica gladly heeded President Juan Rafael Mora's pleas to assemble an army and pay taxes to meet war needs.

When Walker and his filibusters invaded Costa Rica's Guanacaste Province, President Mora and his newly formed army went to meet them. This campaign gave Costa Rica its most romantic national hero. Juan Santamaría, nicknamed Erizo (the Hedgehog), was a drummer boy in Mora's army. In April, 1856, Costa Rican troops caught up with Walker's forces, who were occupying Rivas and using the largest house in town as their headquarters.

Juan Santamaría managed to set fire to the house and rout Walker and his forces. The brave Hedgehog sacrificed his life in this success. In his native Alajuela, stands a splendid statue of the hero, holding his torch aloft.

President Mora and his forces defeated Walker in the Battle of Rosas and other battles, and Mora became the true national hero of his land. The war wore on into 1856, but the greatest damage was done by the fearful epidemic of cholera that swept down from Nicaragua and killed more than ten thousand Costa Ricans, nearly 10 percent of the entire population.

Walker was finally driven out of Nicaragua. When he once again tried to return to Central America and take control, he was captured and shot by a firing squad. Thus ended the strange case of William Walker. According to his biographers, Abdullah and Pakenham, "His dreams of Empire were always petty; always revolving around cheap loot and the adventures themselves."

### A PERIOD OF GROWTH

The Walker events helped to consolidate the country and brought a new wave of patriotism to Costa Rica. This did not immediately mean a more democratic rule, however. A new strong man, General Tomás Guardia, held firm power for ten years. Nevertheless, he did give a new constitution to the people of Costa Rica, which became the basic law of the land for many decades. The country's first really free elections, under this constitution, were held on November 7, 1889.

During the last half of the nineteenth century, Costa Rica made great progress. New products, new means of transportation, and new contacts with the rest of the world contributed to this growth and jobs were plentiful.

Coffee had been introduced into Costa Rica from Cuba as early as 1808. In fact, Costa Rica was the first country of Central America to grow coffee. By 1850, a sub-

**PAN AMERICAN UNION**

Statue of Juan Santamaría, the heroic drummer boy in Mora's army who sacrificed his life to set fire to Walker's headquarters and rout the enemy.

stantial amount of coffee was being exported from Costa Rica.

Costa Rica also pioneered in the banana industry. In 1878, Costa Rica became the first Central American country to raise bananas commercially. The industry grew rapidly on both coasts.

Lack of transportation hindered both the coffee and banana industries. The building of railroads and the beginning of roads helped to enlarge the economy of the country. Coffee from the plantations had to be shipped down the poor mountain roads to the port of Puntarenas in the picturesque but lumbering oxcarts of the countryside. From there it had to be taken by ship around Cape Horn to eastern United States and European markets.

For twenty years, Costa Rica had been trying to build a railroad from San José to Limón, most of it following the valley of the Reventazón River. The jungle-covered slopes, cut by deep valleys that had to be bridged, made railroad building seem almost impossible until an American with the improbable name of Minor Cooper Keith took over the job. "Where a river goes a railroad can go," he vowed.

When Keith ran out of funds, he began to grow bananas along the railroad right-of-way to help pay expenses. This was the beginning of the United Fruit Company and of Keith's personal fortune. The railroad was finally completed in 1890, and Costa Rican coffee and bananas flowed into the markets of the world.

In the early days of Costa Rica's coffee industry, transporation was very poor. Coffee from the plantations had to be shipped down the poor mountain roads to the port of Puntarenas in the picturesque, but lumbering, oxcarts of the countryside.

PAN AMERICAN COFFEE BUREAU

PAN AMERICAN UNION

By 1909 the Pacific port of Puntarenas (above) had been connected by railroad to San José.

# Costa Rica Today

### MODERN TIMES

The "modern" period of Costa Rican life began with the railroad and with the constitution of 1889. Since that time, Costa Rica has had governments that were increasingly under the control of the people. There were some exceptions, such as the coup d'état managed in 1917 by Federico Tinoco, who took over the government of President Alfredo González.

Generally, too, economic conditions have continued to improve, especially with the constant growth of transportation. By 1909 the Pacific port of Puntarenas had been connected by railroad to San José.

The next year saw one of the great disasters of the country. Cartago, the former capital, was destroyed by an earthquake that leveled many of its buildings.

After 1917 only one other break occurred in the democratic processes of Costa Rica. The turbulent presidential campaign and election of 1948 set the scene for revolution. The government candidate lost the election to Otilio Ulate Blanco. The results of the election were disputed by the losing party, and the Legislative Assembly, which had supported the government candidate, voided the election of Ulate, who then fled the country.

José Figueres, a wealthy farmer, led a successful revolt in protest of the Assembly's action. A junta, with Figueres at its head, governed the country until November of 1949. At that time a new constitution took effect and Ulate was finally inaugurated as president. He served his full four-year term under that constitution, the same one that has been in effect ever since.

One of the most unusual provisions of the constitution was to abolish the armed forces, giving Costa Rica the world's only government that is forbidden to form an army.

Since the 1948 revolution and the new constitution, there have been five presidential elections. Though each election rejected the party in power, orderly government continued. In 1970 José Figueres Ferrer, known as "Don Pepe" assumed the presidency, taking over from retiring President José Joaquín Trejos Fernández.

Recent years have witnessed a number of special events of particular interest. In 1960, the National Theater in San José was the meeting place for the ministers of foreign affairs of the American Republics, a part of the Organization of American States. In 1965 the National Theater was declared a national monument.

The increasing attention paid to Costa Rica by the world is indicated by several recent visits of distinguished persons from the United States. President John F. Kennedy visited Costa Rica in 1963, and President Lyndon B. Johnson in 1968. It is an interesting commentary on the peacefulness of Costa Rica that the country had to borrow a cannon from Panama with which to give Mr. Johnson the traditional twenty-one-gun salute.

Not so peaceful or so pleasant was the visit of Nelson A. Rockefeller as special representative of President Richard M. Nixon. During this visit in May, 1969, university students called Rockefeller "proconsul of Emperor Nixon," trampled and burned two American flags, and stoned the United States-Costa Rica Binational Cultural Center.

## DISTINGUISHED COSTA RICANS

José Figueres, sometimes called "Don Pepe," took office in 1970 as president of Costa Rica. This man, who has been dubbed *El Enano*, the Dwarf, because of his short stature, is also known as one of the giants of Latin American politics. He has been called "the grand old man of Latin America's democratic reformers." Figueres had headed his country twice before—in 1948 as dominant member of the junta that ruled after the revolution and again from 1953 to 1958 as president. Responding to criticism that at sixty-three he was too old to hold the office of president, Don Pepe made more than eight hundred speeches in the campaign and received many more votes than all four of his opponents together.

Outstanding artists of Costa Rica include the Spanish painter Tomás Podevano. For nearly fifty years, from its founding in 1897, he directed the School of Fine Arts of Costa Rica. The first Costa Rican artist to be trained in Europe was Enrique Echandi. Internationally known are sculptors Juan Rafael Chacón and Juan Manuel Sánchez, Paco Zeledón, Hernán González, and painter Francisco Amighetti. Other artists prominent in the earlier part of the century are sculptor

José "Pepe" Figueres holds aloft a broom to show that he swept away the opposition in the election of 1970. Figueres received many more votes in this election than all four of his opponents together.

WIDE WORLD PHOTOS

**COSTA RICA**
PROVINCES

Juan Portugués and painters Flora Luján, Margarita Berthaud, Federico Quirós, Manuel Salazar, and Manuel de la Cruz González.

Perhaps the best known Costa Rican artist is Max Jiménez, who was also a writer. He perhaps has best portrayed the artistic atmosphere of the land where he was born. Jiménez is known for the strength of line and exaggeration of form in his work.

In the more modern period, prominent artists include Luis Deel, Oscar Bakit, Lola Fernández, Emilio Willie, Harold Fonseca, and César Valverde.

Many Costa Rican writers are well known in Spanish-speaking lands, including Juan Garita, the priest-poet, and Manuel Argüello Mora, and Arturo Agüero, all of whom wrote in the *Costumbrismo* style.

One of Costa Rica's most versatile writers was Roberto Brenes Mesén, who was also a prominent educator. Aquileo J. Echeverría is generally considered the "National Poet" of Costa Rica. He wrote a series of folk sketches which describe the people of Costa Rica. He was also a diplomat and a journalist. Echeverría is best known for his volume of poetry called *Concherias* (Country Folkways).

A more recent poet of prominence is Alfredo Cardona Peña, author of many volumes of published verse.

Present day Costa Rica is written about in a realistic style by Fabián Dobles, author of *El Sitio de las Abras*. Foremost critic and authority on Costa Rican literature is Abelardo Bonilla.

Music composition in the modern style is done by Julio Mata Creamuno. He is perhaps best known for his *Suite Abstracta,* for symphony orchestra. Noted for his religious compositions is Rafael Chávez Torres. His most famous work is *El Duelo de la Patria*. Also well-known for his church works is Alejandro Monestel, who composes popular tunes as well. A symphony on Costa Rican themes, *Fantasia Sinfónica,* is a prominent work of Julio Fonseca Gutiérrez, while César A. Nieto is known for his ballet *La Piedra del Toxil.*

Other musicians include pianist Guillermo Aguilar Machado, director of the National Conservatory of Music, violinist Raúl Cabezas Duffner, and Daniel Zuñiga, a collector and popularizer of national folk music.

## THE GOVERNMENT OF COSTA RICA

The form of government in Costa Rica is that of a democratic constitutional republic, operating under the constitution of 1949. The national government is divided into three branches, the legislative, the executive, and the judicial. The one-house (unicameral) Legislative Assembly has considerable power. It is composed of fifty-seven deputies, elected for four-year terms. The number of deputies representing a province is determined by provincial population. Deputies are forbidden to succeed themselves in a consecutive term.

The president is relatively limited in his power and authority, but he remains a commanding figure. The president and two vice presidents are elected for four-year terms, and they cannot succeed themselves or return to office until eight years have passed since their last term.

The court system is headed by a Supreme Court of Justice, with seventeen magistrates. The magistrates are elected for eight-year terms by the Legislative Assembly. Lower courts are established by law.

Costa Rica is somewhat unique in the fact that several agencies are permitted to operate almost entirely independently of other governmental authority. Among these are the Social Security Agency, the commercial banks, and the state insurance monopoly.

All citizens over twenty years of age are required to vote in the elections.

There are no legislatures in the individual provinces. These divisions of government are headed by governors appointed by the president, and the provinces are subdivided into regions which are further subdivided into cantons and districts.

## EDUCATION

Costa Rica's high regard for education is one of the principal reasons that Costa Rica has a high standard of living compared to many other Latin American nations. Because Costa Rica has had a free primary school system since 1853, the country now can boast that 85 percent of the people can read and write—the highest percentage in all of Central America and one of the highest in the hemisphere.

Over a third of the national budget is given over to education, compared to only 4 percent for police and national defense. Costa Ricans have long boasted that they have more teachers than policemen. Now they say they are almost ready to boast that they have more school buildings than policemen.

Elementary school in Costa Rica differs very little from that in the United States. It is free, and all children must attend. Secondary school is also free, but attendance is not required.

Until fairly recently the only secondary schools were in the populous Central Valley. Since 1946, however, there have been secondary schools in every province. There are more than a hundred high schools and vocational centers. Since 1944 both primary and secondary schools have required students to study the English language, as well as Spanish.

The government operates many special schools, including evening schools at both the elementary and secondary level and a school of commerce. The law requires special schools, also, for physically and mentally handicapped children. Typical of these is the School of Special Instruction at San José, which provides handicapped children with the skills for trades and other occupations. One of the most interesting specialized schools is Escuela de Tejidos, the school of weaving at Alajuela.

Left: Carlos Melendez, curator of the National Museum, holds the attention of a group of schoolchildren as he explains the history of one of the objects in the museum's collection.
Below: First graders at work in classroom. Costa Rica has had a free primary school system since 1853.

UNITED FRUIT COMPANY

PAN AMERICAN UNION

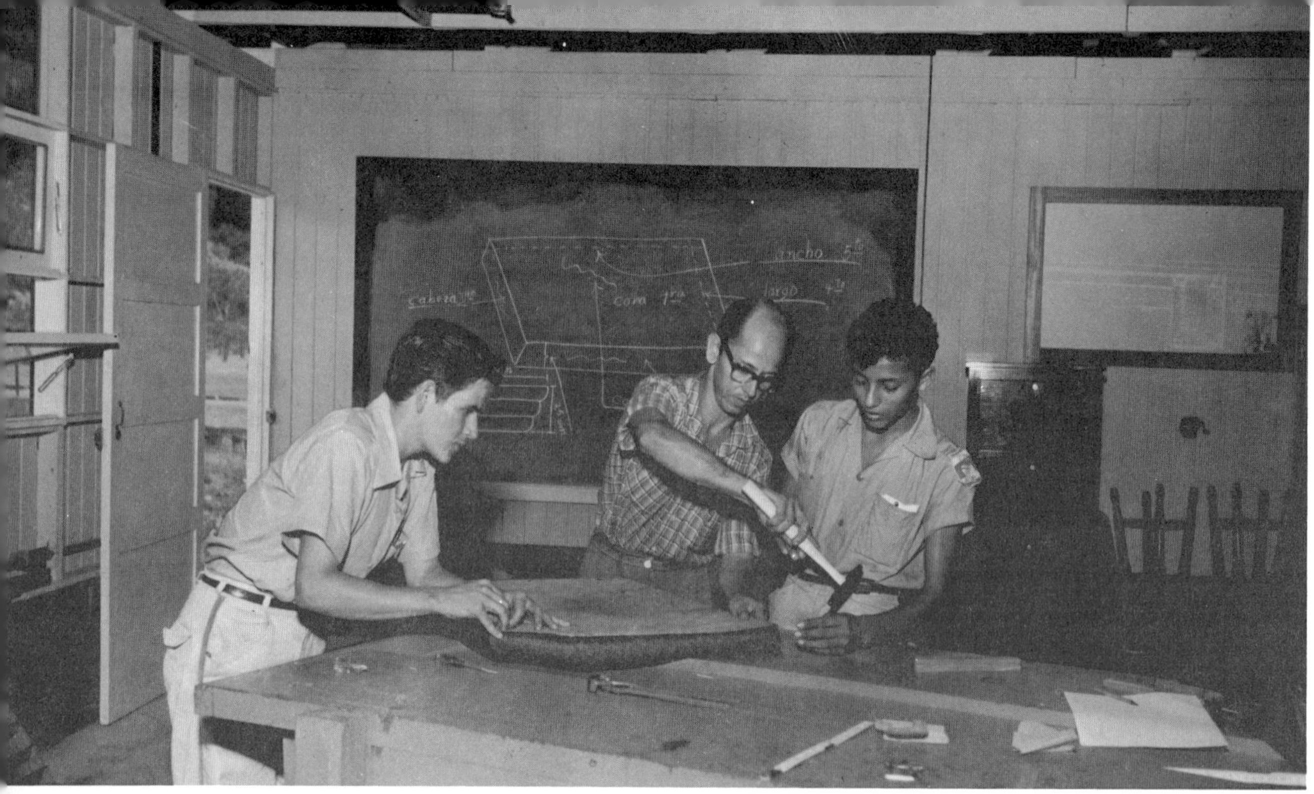

ICA

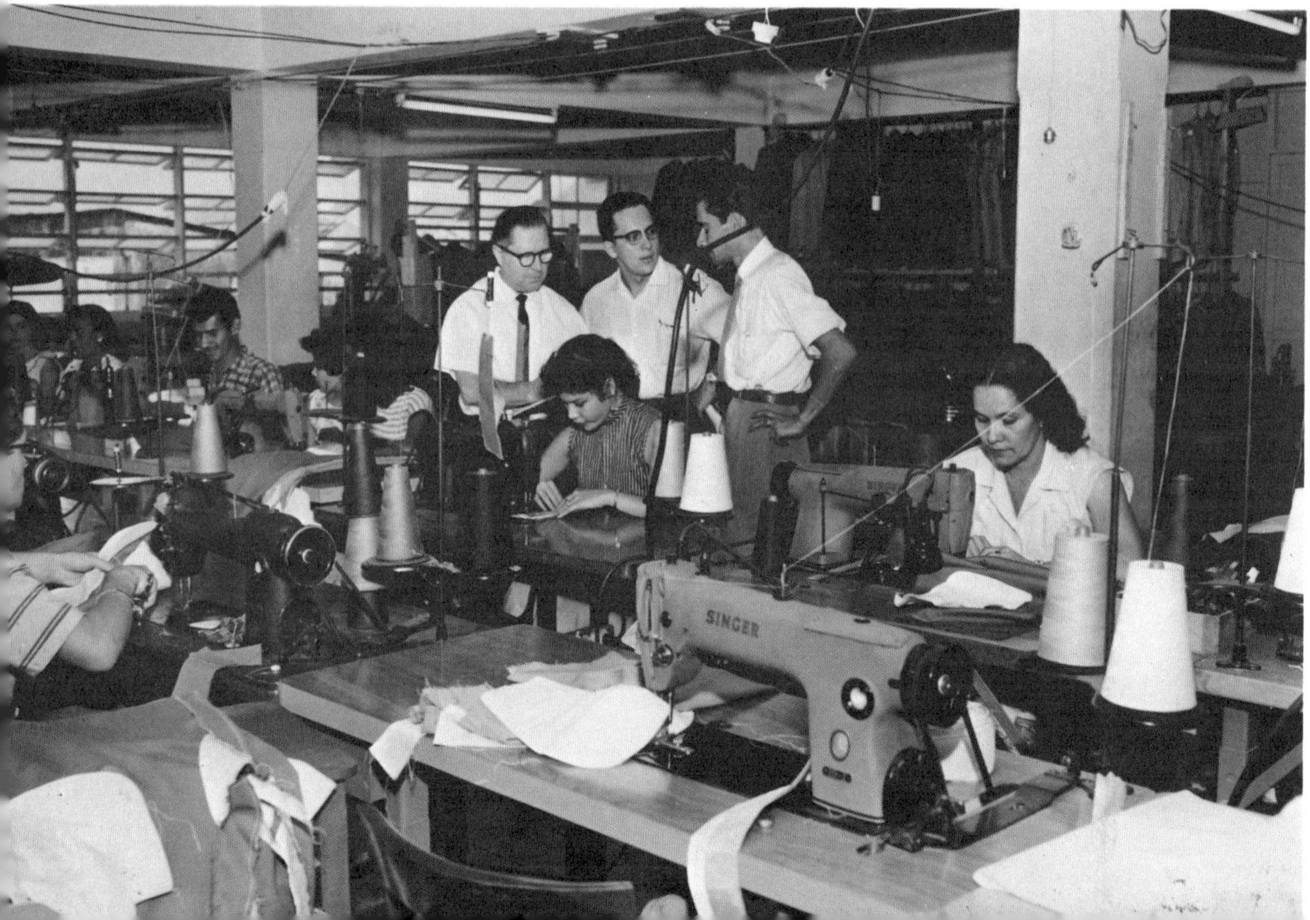


ICA

Opposite, top: Vocational school furniture upholstery class at work.
Opposite, bottom: Vocational school tailoring class. There are more than a hundred high schools and vocational schools in Costa Rica.
Right: Primary students learn good sportsmanship.
Below: Secondary school 4-S Club girls show off their embroidery.

PAN AMERICAN UNION

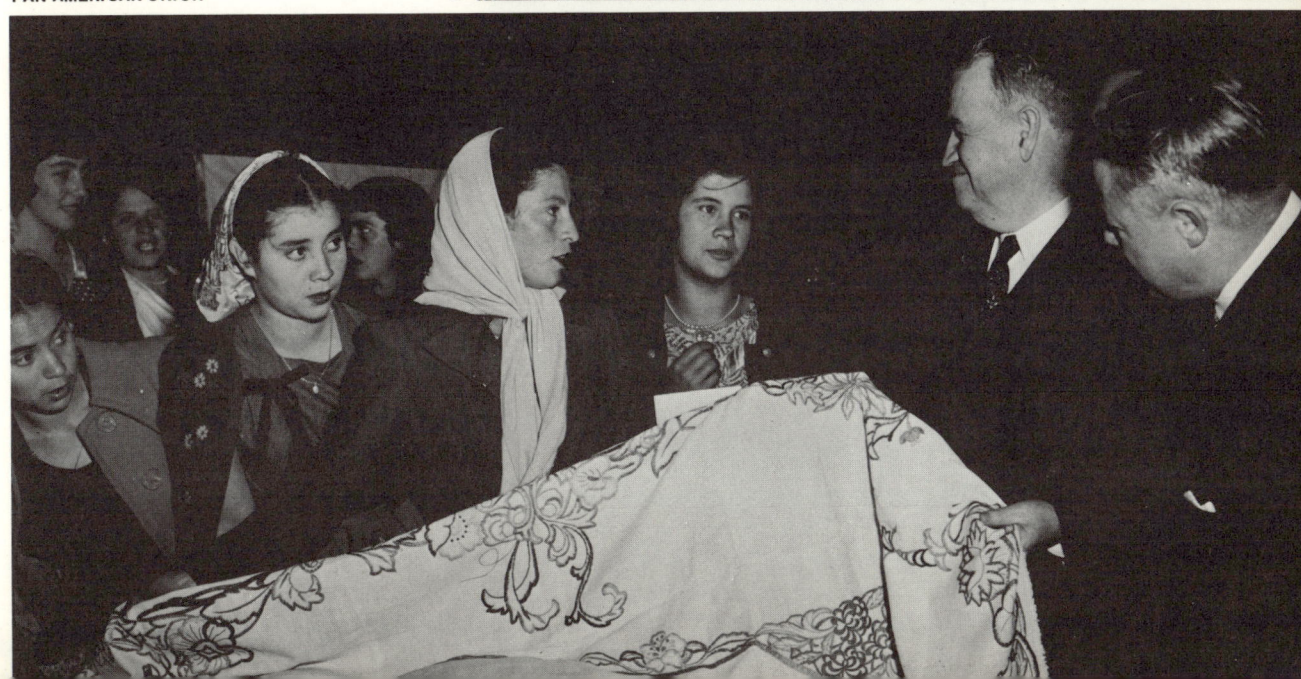

UNITED FRUIT COMPANY

There are also a number of private schools.

The foremost center of learning in Costa Rica is the University of Costa Rica located in the San José suburb of San Pedro de Montes de Oca. It has a faculty of nearly five hundred who teach about nine thousand students in schools of agronomy, microbiology, odontology, music, science and letters, law, economics, medicine, engineering, fine arts, and education.

There are normal schools for the training of teachers at Heredia, Liberia and San Ramón. These enroll a total of about two thousand students. Oldest institution of its kind in the country is the College of San Luis Gonzaga, a trade school directed by the Catholic Salesian order.

Costa Rica can boast one of the finest schools of its kind—the Inter-American Institute of Agricultural Sciences at Turrialba, east of Cartago. The Institute was established by the Organization of American States to provide a place where all the people of the hemisphere could be taught the methods of modern agriculture.

Below: School of Education, National University of Costa Rica near San José. Opposite: In the lobby of one of the university buildings a decorated oxcart has a place of honor.

FOTO CARILLO

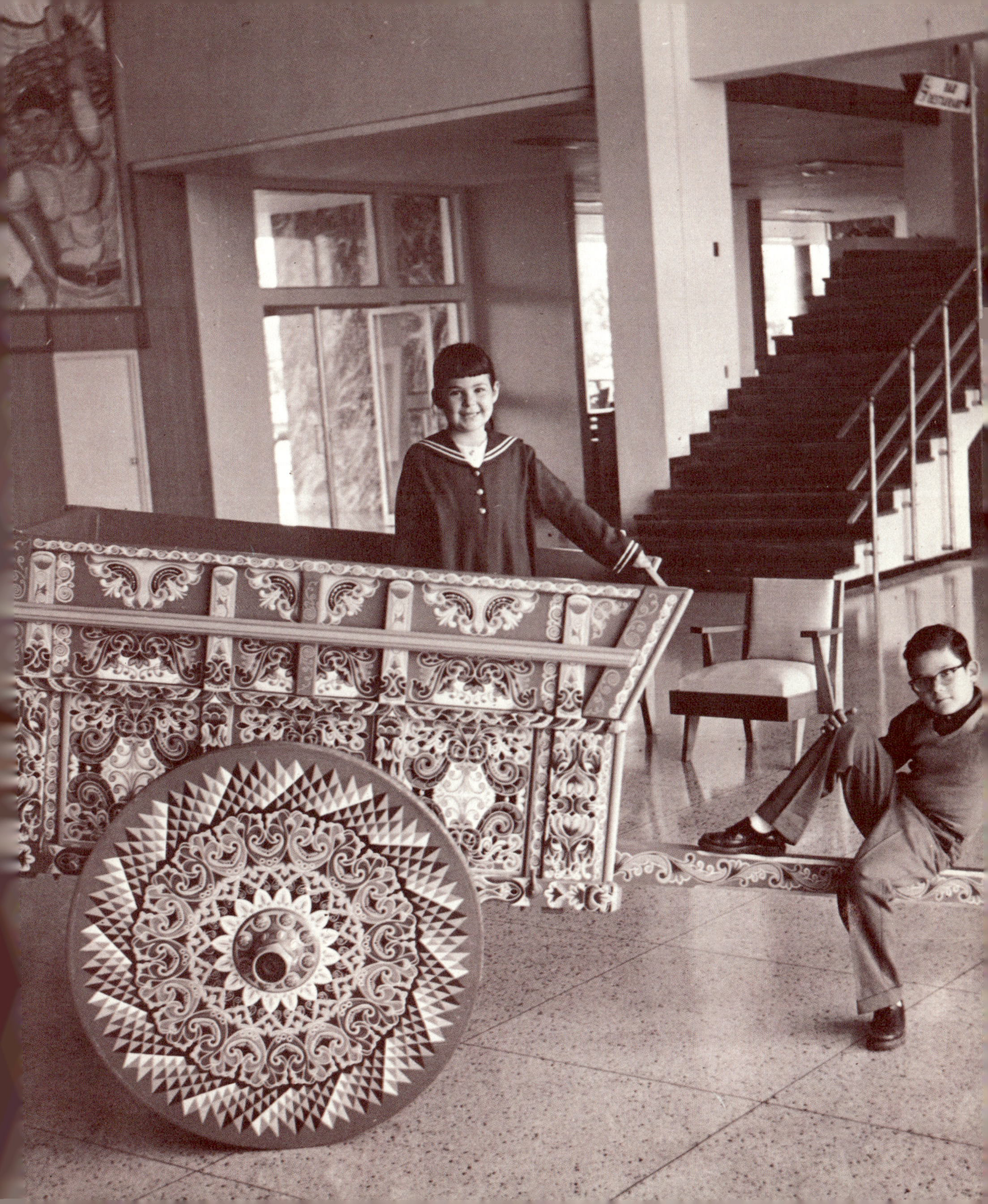

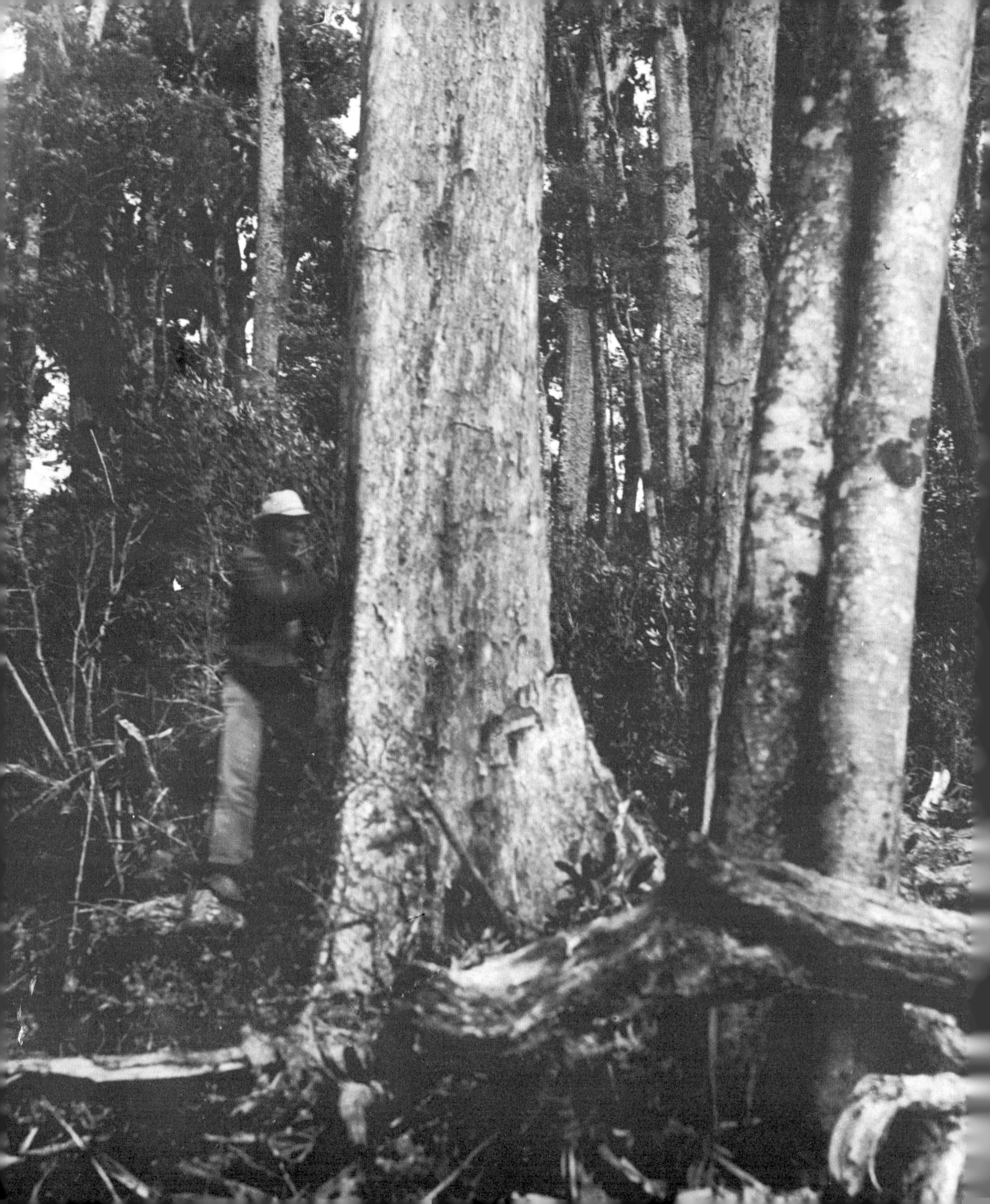

# Natural Treasures

### GROWING THINGS

One of the greatest of Costa Rica's natural resources, perhaps the most valuable of all those known at the present time, is the tremendous covering of trees. Vast forests blanket as much as two thirds of the country.

Most of the Caribbean Coast is covered with woodland swamp forest. Dense woodland extends over much of the rest of the eastern and northern portions of the country. Most of the southeast section also has dense forest cover. To the northwest and southeast of Limón extends a region of valuable trees, interspersed with crop lands.

Much of Guanacaste Province is made up of open woodland. In the southeast more open woodlands lie between the forested regions of each coast. Smaller and scattered forest and woodland areas are found in various other parts of the country.

One of the most interesting trees of Costa Rica is the *guayacán,* a type of lignum vitae native to Guanacaste Province. Sometimes the guayacán grows to be so large and wide spreading that a large herd of cattle can find shelter under the branches of one tree.

Guanacaste Province is well known for its variety of trees and plants; the province covers three climatic zones and offers

---

Among the many types of trees that help make up one of Costa Rica's most valuable natural resources are oak and cenizo (opposite).

**U.S. FOREST SERVICE**

much of interest to naturalists from the world over.

The national tree of Costa Rica is known as *el guanacaste,* whose technical name is enterolobium cyclocarpum. The national flower is the *Guaria Morada,* or cattleye skineri.

### LIVING THINGS

Most glamorous and elusive, and now the rarest of the animal life of Costa Rica, is the magnificent jaguar. This wonderful beast has been driven almost to extinction by hunters who pursue the beautiful animal relentlessly. Often the odds against the jungle creature are made even higher by the use of howling dog packs that track the prey for the hunters. Unfortunately, in spite of its diminished numbers, the jaguar is still being hunted in Costa Rica.

Much of the same animal life found in the humid jungles of the rest of the hemisphere is also found in Costa Rica. The indolent sloth hangs sleepily from branches in many regions. Peccary (the wild pig), tapir, deer, saino, puma and ocelot, tepeiz-cuintle, fox, rabbit, raccoon, wild goat, pizote, muskrat, weasel, and opossum all may be found, and all are prized by hunters.

Hunters also find the land a paradise for many birds, including the king of them all —wild turkey. Other game birds include duck, snipe, quail, wild hen, guinea hen, pigeon (including bandtailed), and purple dove.

Few countries offer fishermen the sport to be found in Costa Rica. In Atlantic offshore waters there are Atlantic and blue marlin, Atlantic sailfish, dolphin, barracuda, amberjack, and wahoo. A particularly tasty fish for the fisherman who enjoys eating his catch is the delicious corbina. The snapper is also much admired as a delicacy. Fish caught off the Pacific shores are Pacific sailfish, Pacific blue marlin, dolphin, shark, manta ray, machaca, bob, sac ete, snook, rainbow runner, and rooster fish.

Inshore fishing includes tarpon and snook. The Atlantic rivers provide trout and muchacha. The latter runs from three to five pounds and is said to act like a baby tarpon after taking the hook.

Commercial types of fish include large numbers of mackerel and tuna.

### MINERALS

The known mineral resources of Costa Rica are not very large. Perhaps the most extensive mineral deposit is bauxite, basic material for aluminum. Largest deposits, estimated at 150 million tons, are found in Rio General Valley. Other bauxite areas include Venecia de San Carlos, an area south of Guacimo, Abajonel Hill, San José Province, and some parts of Puntarenas Province.

Small deposits of sulphur are found at El Congo Hill, Alajuela Province, and northeast of Liberia in Guanacaste Prov-

The Guaria Morada orchid (left) is the national flower of Costa Rica.

**PAN AMERICAN UNION**

The Reina de la Noche, with its great, trumpet-shaped blossoms, is found in most of the republic.

**PAN AMERICAN UNION**

ince. Lignite, zinc, lead, manganese, methane, and salt, all in relatively unimportant quantities, are other minerals found in the country.

Deposits of iron have been found in eight scattered locations, and copper in seven, but again in comparatively small amounts. Gold and silver have been found in several provinces. Only one deposit of petroleum is known. This is in Limón Province and is considered to be non-commercial.

There is a rich asphalt deposit on Caño Island, near the mouth of the Rio Grande de Térraba. The Boruca Indians once used this to seal their canoes.

# The People Live in Costa Rica

### A "DIFFERENT" SPANISH HERITAGE

Of all the nations in the western hemisphere settled by the Spanish, Costa Rica is the only one that was and still is substantially different from all the others. The Spanish settlers found an extremely small Indian population in the entire area. As the years went on, the number of Indians decreased rather than increased. Fiercely independent, the Indian peoples remained aloof from the European settlers, refusing to work for them or even to associate with them. Because Costa Rica was so remote and far away from the main trade routes, it did not seem practical to bring in large numbers of slaves.

Consequently, the Spanish settlers had to do most of the work themselves. Throughout the Spanish period this kept the farms small, one-family operations, with only a few large plantations operated by wealthy landowners. Thus, Costa Rica was the only Spanish land not dominated by a handful of extremely wealthy property owners, who kept most of the people in poverty in many other Spanish lands. Most of the people of Costa Rica were middle-class landowners. This probably is why the democratic tradition is so firmly established in Costa Rica.

Later, as coffee and banana plantations multiplied and grew larger, there came to be a number of large landholders, operating more or less on the traditional plantation system. However, this happened so late that it did not change the general pattern of the country.

Only in the Pacific coastlands of Guanacaste Province was there a minority of people of pure Spanish descent living in large haciendas on enormous cattle estates. That province has always had a way of life quite distinctive from the rest of Costa Rica.

The people there have long lived a life of open-handed hospitality with much attention paid to music and dancing. They gave the nation its official national dance —the punto guanacasteco—and the area is noted for its festivals and merrymaking.

Costa Rica differs from the other former Spanish colonies in still another way. Almost the entire population is of European descent, mostly from Spanish lands. Forty-seven percent of the people are a mixture of bloods, but even in these the European background dominates.

Probably not more than three thousand full-blooded Amerindians (American Indians) remain in all of Costa Rica. They make up less than 1 percent of the popula-

Costa Rica's Talamanca Indians (below) catch fish with bows and arrows.

PAN AMERICAN UNION

Though there are many small, one-family farms in Costa Rica, there are also many large ranches, such as the two coffee plantations shown here.

PAN AMERICAN UNION

A Costa Rican fisherman looks out to sea.

**PAN AMERICAN UNION**

tion. Not much more numerous in proportion to the entire population are the Negroes, who total about 2 percent. Many of these are descendants of West Indian people brought in to help build the railroads. Most of these settled in Limón Province.

### WHERE AND HOW THE PEOPLE LIVE

Costa Rica has the second smallest population in Central America, if only the republics are considered. By far the largest part of the population lives in Meseta Central, the famous Central Valley. Though estimates of the valley population vary between 90 percent of the total and two thirds of the total, everyone agrees that the Central Valley people make up a large part of the whole.

The country has a young population, with more than two thirds of all the people only twenty-four years old or younger. This is a reflection of the fact that Costa Rica's population growth of 4.2 percent per year is one of the world's highest.

Recent figures showed the annual income per person to be 363 dollars per year, the second highest in Central America. Since 1950 the economic and social progress made by the people of Costa Rica has exceeded that of any other Central American country.

The Ministry of Public Health has the responsibility for the mental and physical health of all Costa Ricans. An unusual provision of the constitution requires all sixty-five cities and towns of the nation to spend at least 20 percent of their total income for public health.

Establishment of health centers, particularly in rural areas, has been one of the most notable reasons for an improvement of the general health. Mother and child care, treatment of parasitic diseases and malaria, vaccinations, and other health care are given.

There are nearly forty health centers, regional hospitals, and central hospitals in Costa Rica. At Duran there is a widely known sanitarium that specializes in pulmonary diseases.

Costa Rica is also known for its liberal prison system, and especially for the unique prison at San Lucas Island in the Nicoya Gulf. Here a prisoner lives for a trial period in the prison itself. Then he is given the keys to a place of his own. The

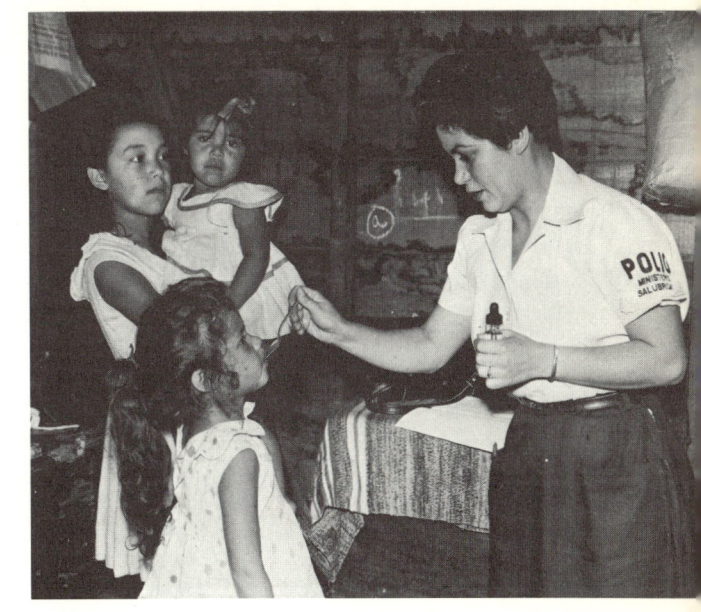

PASB/WHO

The constitution of Costa Rica requires the towns and cities of the nation to spend at least 20 percent of their income for public health. Above: Visiting public welfare nurse administers oral polio vaccine to three sisters. Below: A "company" hospital at Golfito.

UNITED FRUIT COMPANY

prisoners may study to improve themselves, work for a minimum wage, and make items to be sold to tourists. Five days each month wives or friends may visit.

The official state religion in Costa Rica is Roman Catholicism, and a large part of the population professes that faith. However, there are other religious groups. The first Anglican Church in Central America was formed at San José, and there is a prospering colony of Quakers from the United States at Monteverde de Guacinial.

## CUSTOMS

The people of Costa Rica are often called Ticos, and residents of San José are known as Josefinos. Josefinos like to think that among them are the most beautiful women of the world, and some experts on beauty have agreed that they are right.

The people of Costa Rica practice one of the most widely known and unique folk arts anywhere. This is the painting of bright, picturesque designs of many colors, especially on the heavy farm carts pulled by oxen. The intricate geometric designs —no two ever quite alike—that cover the body, wheels, and even the yokes of the carts are painted in vivid colors.

Although not even the sociologists are quite sure how this art originated, the painted carts have had a long tradition in Costa Rica; almost every farmer showed a unique skill in the design he painted on his cart. Each province has its own predominating color.

A good description of this truly distinctive art was given in the national tourist magazine: "The marvelous decoration of the oxcarts in Costa Rica is a strip of color and vibration that elevates the landscape and raptures the eye of the traveler with contrasts. A rose from the winds with a thousand diamonds on each wheel; flowers and color balance on the side panels. Grecian frets and shades everywhere put this work implement in the category of a work of art that makes its owner proud and symbolizes his gentility, generosity, and elegance in knowing how to live . . . a calling card of our countryfolk. The flower Sunday or the town fair becomes a noble competition of designs and the prizes for the best painted oxcart activate more this beautiful and exclusive Costa Rican tradition."

Many Americans are so taken with the farm carts that they buy them and have them shipped home for flower carts and other decorations. Most younger Costa Ricans do not seem to have the patience to learn this painting skill, and so, sadly, the interesting tradition seems to be dying out in the countryside.

Although Costa Rica is not so Spanish in many of its ways, some traditional Spanish colonial customs are found. There are many fiestas; often these finish in the town square with a harmless form of bullfighting in which no horses are used.

Customs of the cattle province of Guanacaste are similar to those of Argentina and Chile and some other South American lands of Spanish origin, chiefly Uruguay. The *asada*, or barbecue, is a popular combination of eating and entertainment. In this wild west of Costa Rica, cowboys still drive their herds of cattle across the savannas.

Even the horses wear traditional "costumes." Each cowboy outfits his horse with the finest saddle he can afford. These are fastened over skirts made of black fleece. Cruppers are decorated with horsehair rosettes and tassels, with bright decorations on the head.

In addition to the national dance, the punto guanacasteco, celebrations often include forms of popular music which are distinctive to Costa Rica. Even some remnants of Indian music have been preserved along with some of the Indian instruments which are still being used. One of these instruments is the ocarina, used by the Huetar people. They produced eighteen notes on an instrument with only six finger holes. The quijongo is a drum made of wood and animal hide. Traditional instruments today include a kind of oboe known as chirimía, the guitar, and the marimba.

San José is noted for the *Retreta*, an old Spanish custom which is dying out in many other parts of Latin America. Three times each week in Central Park girls stroll arm-in-arm around the plaza in one direction while the young men walk in the opposite direction.

As with so many other Latin American countries, soccer is the national sport of Costa Rica. Among other activities, water sports are probably the fastest-growing in popularity.

Coffee seedlings are wrapped carefully before being moved to prepared fields for transplanting.

PAN AMERICAN UNION

When they are at just the right point of ripeness, the coffee berries are picked by hand.

PAN AMERICAN UNION

PAN AMERICAN UNION

The berries are placed in a farm cart to be brought to drying areas.

# The People Work in Costa Rica

The rich volcanic soil, the good climate, and the lush green appearance of the Central Valley all have given Costa Rica its long-time reputation as "garden of the Americas." It is not surprising that Costa Rica is mainly an agricultural country; coffee has long been the principal crop.

Visitors find the coffee *fincas* (farms) fascinating places with the coffee trees growing on the high slopes of the mountains, shaded by taller, sturdier trees. The glistening dark green leaves partially conceal clusters of white waxy flowers. Those not familiar with the way coffee grows are surprised to find blossoms, green coffee berries, and ripe coffee berries growing on the same tree at the same time. At just the right point of ripeness the berries must be picked by hand and placed in the farm carts. Lucky visitors may still find a place where the picturesque hand-painted carts are being used. The coffee is brought to the drying areas, where it is dried in the sun and treated in various ways to make it ready for roasting. Nearly 150 thousand acres in Costa Rica are devoted to coffee raising, with Heredia the center of the coffee industry.

Second most important among Costa Rican crops is the banana. More than ten million bunches are grown there each year. Banana growing in Costa Rica reached its peak in 1913. After that, the yield decreased due to disease. To escape the disease, much of the industry moved to the Pacific Coast of Costa Rica. Now, however, the Caribbean Coast is making a comeback in the banana industry.

Many of the largest growers operate almost completely independent plantation centers, like towns, with stores, schools, and other benefits for workers and families. There are company-owned railroads to bring the bananas to port, and company-owned port facilities to ship them out.

Most staple crops, including potatoes, corn, beans, and sugarcane, grow well in the fertile Central Valley. The cane industry is expanding rapidly in Costa Rica. Alajuela, in the Central Valley, is noted as the "granary of Costa Rica."

Costa Rica grows enough cotton to provide for its own textile industry. Oranges and other citrus fruits flourish. Among the more exotic "crops" are orchids from the famous orchid farms of Costa Rica, such as Las Cóncavas near Paraiso.

The livestock industry of the country is growing and improving rapidly. More than a million cattle now graze on the stock farms along with a substantial and increasing number of hogs. Live cattle and frozen beef already make up Costa Rica's third largest export. Arabian horses are bred in the area around the villages of Navarro and Coris. The dairy industry thrives in the Central Valley, where the large population requires many dairy products.

UNITED FRUIT COMPANY

Left: Bananas, Costa Rica's second most important crop, at a washing station.

Below: Heavily fruited cacao tree.

UNITED FRUIT COMPANY

Costa Rican girl
displays agricultural products
native to her country.

**ICA**

Costa Rica exports
shark liver
from huge fish
such as this one
caught in the waters
off Puntarenas.

**PAN AMERICAN UNION**

Among Costa Rica's small industries are food packing plants such as this tomato packing plant in Cartago.

**PAN AMERICAN UNION**

Sorting and packing tomatoes for shipment.

**PAN AMERICAN UNION**

### INDUSTRIOUS COSTA RICANS

There are no enormous industrial and manufacturing complexes in Costa Rica. Most of the industries are comparatively small and provide products needed by the local people. Many are based on the agricultural products. Typical of these is a modern factory at San José that makes soluble coffee. El Brasil, near Ojo de Agua, is one of Costa Rica's largest coffee-processing plants.

For many years, the number of Costa Rican industries has been increasing rapidly. New industries have included nylon hosiery, fertilizer, textile, paper, oil refining, and automobile assembly plants.

There are many factories for making consumer goods such as cigarettes and cigars, footwear, rubber products, cosmetics, paints, fertilizers, plastics, insecticides, furniture, clothing, and textiles. There is a sizeable food and beverage industry, including a national liquor factory at San

José. Here the government-owned plant produces popular liquors including Cocarí rum and the unique crema de nance.

Products of the sea have not yet played a large part in Costa Rica's economy. However, there are some commercial fishing enterprises such as the small tuna fishing industry based at Puntarenas. Some pearls and mother of pearl are also harvested from the Gulf of Nicoya.

The vast forests of Costa Rica have barely been touched by the lumber industry. Cativo, a kind of soft wood from which plywood is made, and cedar have been cut to some extent. However, the enormous resources of the forests remain still to be tapped.

The same is true of the mineral resources, which are not nearly so rich as the forests. The construction industry takes most of the mineral production of Costa Rica. Building stones, such as marble, serpentine, travertine, and limestone are quarried and finished for construction. Limestone, glass sand, and asbestos are also produced. Cement plants and other processers transform those raw materials into items used by the building trade.

There is still a small industry of gold and silver mining in several provinces. Minor salt-evaporating activities in Puntarenas and Guanacaste provinces just about round out the mineral productivity of present Costa Rica.

Costa Rica has fifty-seven electric generating plants. Of these, thirty-five generate with hydroelectric power.

The latest figures show that Costa Rica imported goods worth about 180 million dollars, while the exported goods totaled only about 140 million dollars. This means that Costa Rica has what is called an unfavorable balance of trade, buying more than it is able to sell.

Coffee accounts for nearly 50 percent of all Costa Rican exports, bananas about 25 percent, followed by cattle, sugar, and cacao.

## TRANSPORTATION

Costa Rica is easily reached by all major forms of transportation. Visitors and cargo can come or go by car, bus, or truck from either north or south on the Pan American Highway. Many scheduled airlines and air freight companies carry people and goods to Costa Rica, while several excellent ports handle millions of tons of freight.

## WATER TRANSPORTATION

Although they do not handle any regularly scheduled passenger transportation, the ports are perhaps most important of all to Costa Rica. There are four major ports. Three of the principal ports of the country are located on the Pacific side.

Puntarenas ranks second in imports and also exports cattle, sugar, coconuts, canned fish, and such shark products as oil

**UNITED FRUIT COMPANY**

and skins. Golfito, the United Fruit port, handles more export freight than any other port of the country. Its principal shipment, of course, is bananas. Golfito also ranks third among the ports in imports. The third important Pacific port is Quepos, also built by United Fruit for banana handling. A fourth, smaller, port is Caldera.

Still the single most important port, Limón is the only one of any consequence on the Atlantic side. That ancient city has long been one of Costa Rica's major contacts with the rest of the world. It continues to handle the greatest total tonnage of the Costa Rican ports.

There is much coastwise shipping on both the Pacific and Atlantic sides, as well as some shipment up major inland waterways. The coastal and inland waterway fleet of Costa Rica consists of sixty-two vessels owned by twenty-eight shipping companies. The most important movement of traffic occurs on the PacificCoast where twenty-one individual companies operate forty vessels with a combined tonnage of about a thousand long tons.

The ships move between several of the Pacific ports and also as far north as Nicaragua. Freight is carried up the Tempisque River as far as Bolson.

On the Atlantic side, several of the connecting rivers serve a number of far inland cities. Atlantic coastal shipping moves from Limón to the small ports of Barrade Colorado and Punta Cahuila.

---

Bananas being loaded into the hold of a ship at Golfito, the United Fruit port.

## AVIATION

When it was built several years ago, Costa Rica's largest airport, El Coco, was the biggest and most modern in Central America. Still among the most convenient in Latin America, it is only about ten miles away from San José by superhighway and is even closer to Alajuela. La Sabana Airport, on the outskirts of San José, is used for domestic flights.

Costa Rica has sixteen other airports for domestic flying. The largest of these is at Limón. Others are Sabana, Chacarita, Golfito, Nicoya, Santa Cruz, Parrita, Buenos Aires, La Cañas, Palmar Sur, Volcán, Upsala, San Vito de Java, Liberia, Guápiles, and Los Chiles.

Several major airlines serve as links between Costa Rica and other countries. The main domestic airline is LACSA, the national airline of the country. Other local lines are COPA, PAA, SAHSA, and TACA.

## HIGHWAYS

A substantial link of one of the world's major highways cuts through the length of

Air field at Santa Cruz, one of Costa Rica's seventeen airports used only for domestic flying.

STANDARD OIL OF NEW JERSEY

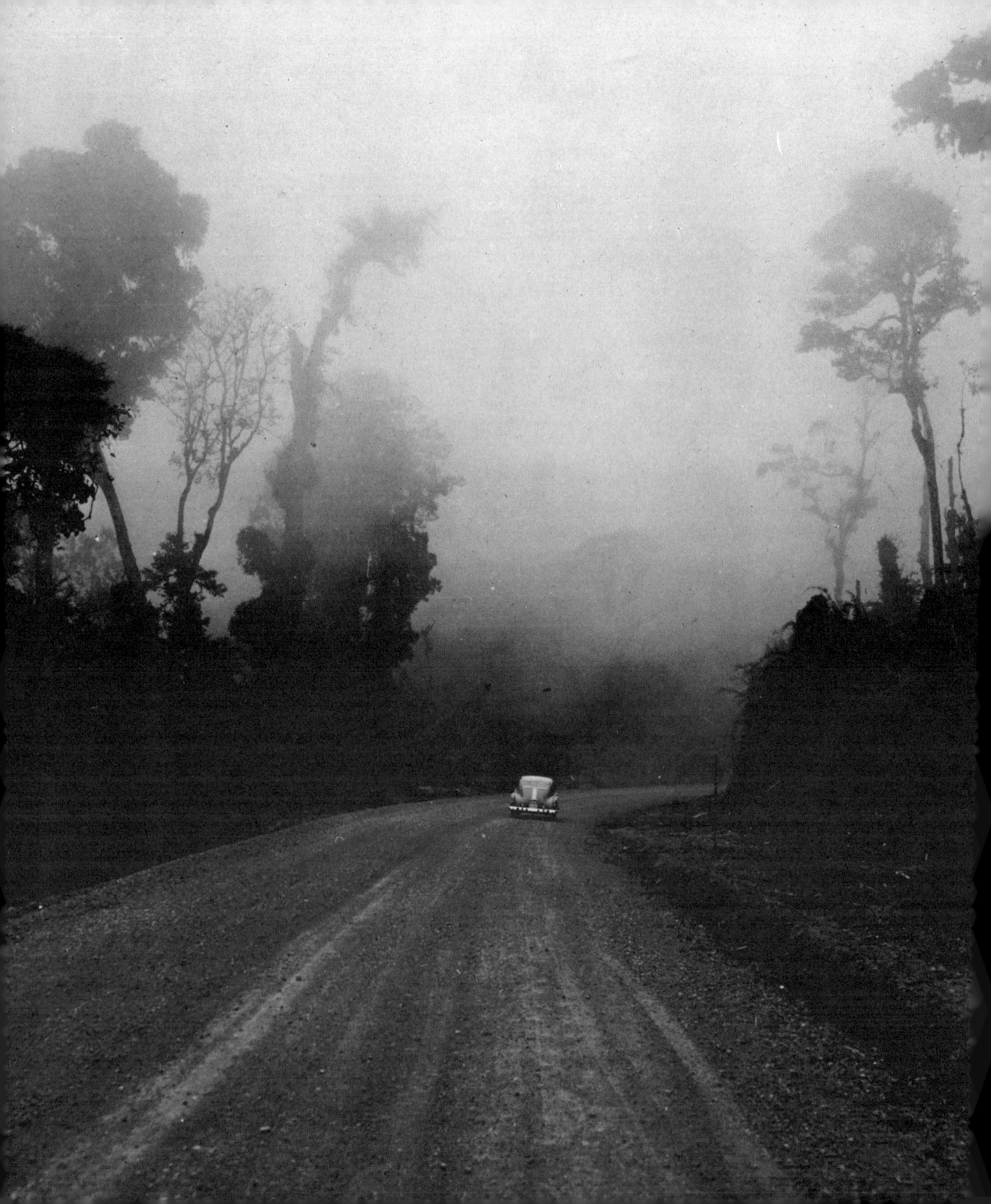

Opposite and above: Scenes on Costa Rica's stretch of the Pan American Highway.   **PAN AMERICAN UNION**

Costa Rica. This is the great Pan American Highway, which connects Costa Rica by road with points between the United States-Mexican border and Panama City. When the final link of the highway is completed in southern Panama, the road will be open all the way to southern Chile and Argentina.

In the highlands south of San José, the Pan American Highway hits its highest point between Texas and Panama, reaching an elevation of 10,931 feet. The section from San Isidro to Panama is the only portion of the great highway in Central America that is still unpaved. There is good bus service from San José to Guatemala City and Panama City.

A highway map of Costa Rica shows a cluster of good roads in the Central Valley and several leading from the Central Valley to other parts of the country. There is a highway that connects San José with Puntarenas, on the Pacific, and another highway that connects San José with Limón, on the Atlantic. A highway also extends down much of the length of the central Nicoya Peninsula. Altogether there are about five hundred miles of paved roads in Costa Rica and about twelve hundred miles of other all-weather roads.

## RAILROADS

As noted before, the coming of the railroads probably did more to modernize Costa Rica than any other one thing. The building of the railroad from Limón to

San José was one of the most difficult feats in the history of construction. The first twenty-five miles of construction is said to have taken a toll of four thousand lives, mostly of Chinese laborers brought in to do the work. The road required nineteen years to complete. It opened up a new era of communication between the populous Central Valley and the markets to the east.

An electric railroad now links San José with Puntarenas, so that Costa Rica is linked by railroad from coast to coast. San José and Alajuela are connected by passenger railroad. There is also passenger service from Limón to the towns of Atlanta and Toro Amarillo.

Altogether there are about eight hundred miles of railroad in Costa Rica. However, six hundred miles of this trackage is privately owned; most of these tracks are on the plantations to provide market transportation for bananas and coffee. One of these private railroads runs from Golfito to the left bank of the Rio Grande de Térraba, across the river from the landing at the Puerto de Coto, and from Golfito to the border with Panama. In addition to Golfito, other towns served are Puerto Cortés, Palmar Sur, Piedras Blancas, Unión de Coto, Corredor, and Laurel.

Even more remote is the railroad which carries bananas from the plantations to Sixaola in the far southeastern part of the country. Smallest of the railroads is Ferrocarril de Quepos, which serves that town and Parrita on the Pacific.

## COMMUNICATIONS

Leading newspapers of San José are *La Republica, La Nacion,* and *El Diario de Costa Rica,* all published in the morning, and the evening papers *La Hora* and *La Prensa Libre.*

Telephone service is somewhat limited by standards of the North. Fewer than ten thousand residences in the entire country have telephones and most of these are in the capital city. Fewer than five thousand of the country's businesses have the advantage of a telephone.

A network of telegraph lines serves much of the country. Remote towns are in contact only through radio-telephone. There are cable connections with Panama and Nicaragua.

# Enchantment of Costa Rica

Costa Rica is a beautiful country with springlike weather, vivid green foliage covering lofty mountains, multi-hued flowers blanketing much of the countryside, and valleys cut by sparkling rivers.

Tourists are attracted not only by the beauty of the country, but also by the marvelous fishing and hunting, the swimming at modern beach resorts and attractive spas, the warm tropical sun, the invigorating cool of the mountains, the comfortable lodging in most areas, and the many restaurants offering good and unusual foods.

## ENCHANTING SAN JOSÉ

The traveler who arrives at El Coco International Airport and takes a cab into San José may expect one of the bumpy, dusty interminable rides over bad or partly repaired roads that are typical of airport roads in so much of Latin America. Instead, he flashes onto a fine four-lane highway and is whisked off to the heart of the city. The narrow roads and the picturesque painted oxcarts for which Costa Rica is famous will come later in his visit.

Lack of these unique vehicles on the streets of San José may disappoint him, but a few are still to be found lumbering over the back roads of the countryside. Duplicates can be bought in some of the craft shops of San José. These reproductions are now manufactured in great numbers for tourist souvenirs. They are covered with the famous designs of the original carts. The souvenir carts range in size from toys two or three inches long to life-size models that can be used for flower carts or bars.

The larger ones can be dismantled for shipment. Although many tourists feel that they are too slick and polished looking and would prefer to buy an original farm cart, this is almost impossible.

The craft shops of San José display a wealth of other craft souvenirs hand made by the people of Costa Rica or surrounding countries, but nothing is quite as distinctive as the carts.

## MAGNIFICO!

In addition to the carts, the tourist probably has heard about the great National Theater (Teatro Nacional) building. This extraordinary structure fully lives up to its advance billing as one of the two finest opera houses in all of Latin America; it is smaller, but perhaps no less magnificent, than the huge opera house of Buenos Aires.

The front of the building, in classical Renaissance architectural style, is the work of Costa Rican stonecutters. Stone statues at the top symbolizing the Dance, Music, and Fame, were sculptured by Italian master Pietro Bulgarelli. There are also statues of Beethoven and Spanish author Calderón de la Barca.

The striking vestibule has marble columns in Pompeiian style, topped with bronze capitals. The marble floor is in a beautiful mosaic pattern. Statues by Costa Rican sculptor Juan Ramón Bonilla guard the inner doors. The lavish main staircase has ornaments of gold leaf and enormous ornate candelabra of bronze. Both the steps and railings are of various shades of marble. A mural glorifying coffee and bananas was painted by José Villa of Milan.

Perhaps the most truly beautiful room in the building is the magnificent foyer. The ceiling is decorated with gorgeous mural paintings representing Dawn, Day, and Night; they were done by Italian painter Luigi Vignani, who later did the Moscow Opera House murals. The marble of various kinds and colors used in the room, the gleaming parquet wood floors from the finest Costa Rican woods, the majestic marble columns, the beautifully designed, carved, and decorated furniture, and the gold laminated ornaments were combined in a way that forms a perfectly integrated effect.

The main auditorium is a classic horseshoe shape with four levels of seating; a dazzling mural by Arturo Fontana and an enormous sparkling crystal chandelier add grandeur to the theater. The pit of the stage was unusual for its time, since it can be raised to the level of the stage, increasing the stage space for ballroom or conference use.

## PLEASANT CITY

In its location, San José is almost ideal. The altitude of 3,870 feet in the beautiful broad Central Valley gives it warm days

Magnificent interior of Costa Rica's National Theater. No tourist to San José should miss seeing this remarkable building.

ERNST A. JAHN

and cool evenings; the rainy season is mild, lasting from May to November.

Although founded in 1737, San José did not become the capital until 1823. Many observers say that the city is the least Spanish of any of the capitals of Latin America. Most of the houses are in the style of North America or of European nations other than Spain.

Though streets are generally wide and laid out at straight angles, visitors often have difficulty finding a location in San José because of the confusing numbers and names of the streets, which seem to change from block to block.

In mid-course the main street, Avenida Central, changes its name to the Paseo Colón, named to honor Christopher Columbus. Along the Colón are some of the finest residences of the city, many of them in chalet style.

Paseo Colón leads to La Sabana, once the national airport and now home of the Costa Rican Tourist Institute and the large stadium. The main former airport building, in the old Spanish-Moorish style,

Above: Children's park in San José. Opposite: Crowded, narrow street in downtown San José seems to lead directly to the mountains in the distance.

has hand-carved mahogany doors, carved beamed ceilings, and wrought-iron railings and grilles.

There are many fine parks in and around the city. Bolívar Park honors Simón Bolívar, hero of South America. Its zoo has many fine examples of the animals and birds of Central America. The National Lottery is held in the Central Park every other Sunday to benefit the hospitals of the country.

Four large gardens meet at a splendid temple of music in Morazán Park; this temple is also a bandstand. National Park is noted for its monument dedicated to the other Central American countries.

## DOWNTOWN SAN JOSÉ

The modern San José city hall faces Merced Park. Here also is a huge stone carved into a sphere by some prehistoric race that is completely unknown to modern man.

The Metropolitan Cathedral faces a pleasant parklike square in the heart of the city. The cathedral is not a particularly imposing building, although its clean and simple lines give it a quiet dignity that seems appropriate to the city. Here each Sunday, men of the Military Band of Costa Rica go to eight o'clock Mass in their full dress uniforms to worship and

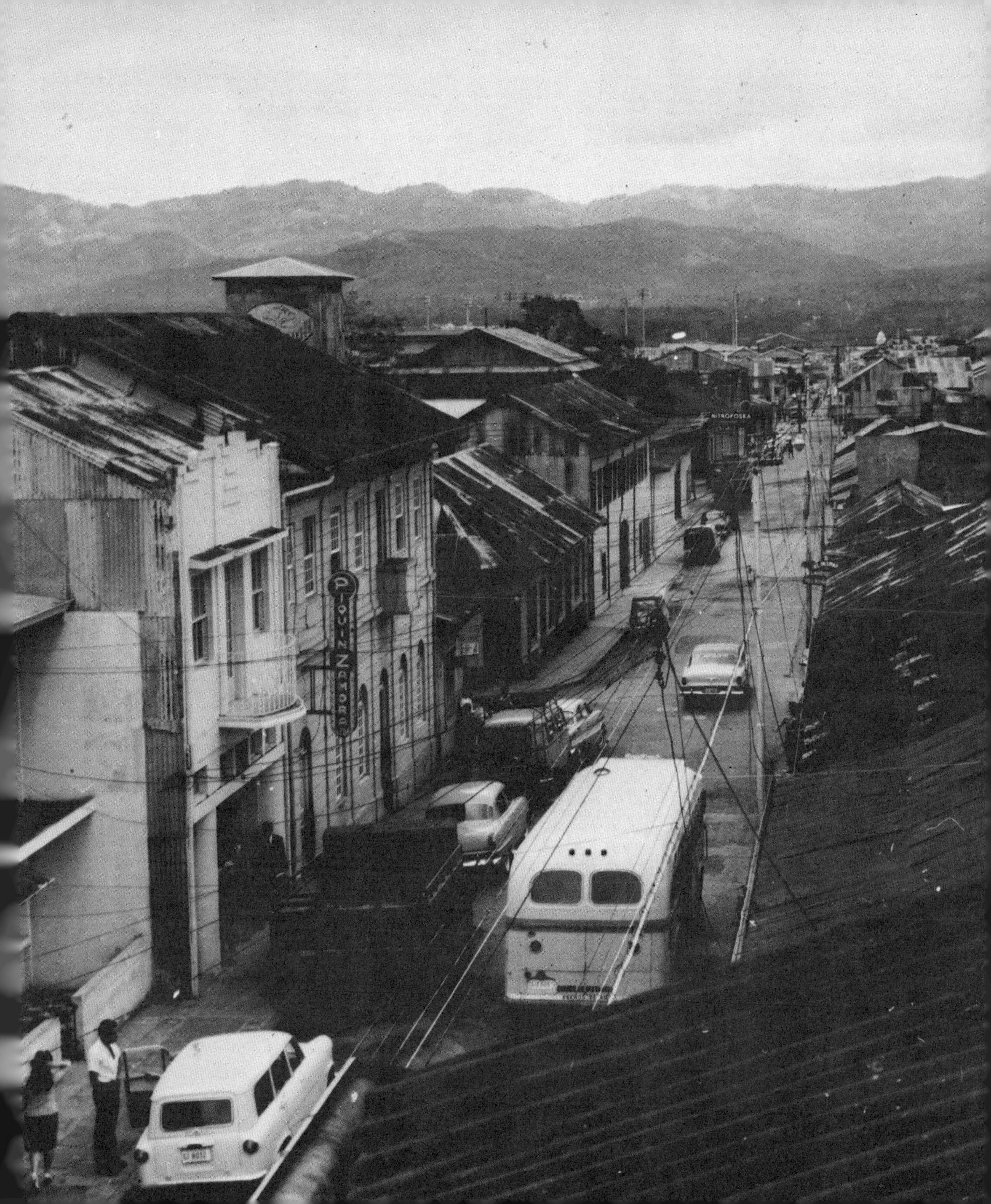
PIQUIN ZAMORA
NITROFOSKA

hear the choir which is noted for the quality of its music.

Other downtown churches include La Soledad, Los Dolores, and El Carmen. The Anglican Church, founded in 1864, was the first of its kind to be established in Central America.

Located on Avenida Central is the Legislative Assembly building. It is especially well known for its collection of fine portraits of the presidents of Costa Rica and other prominent public figures.

Another principal point of interest is the National Museum. Its building once was the main fortification of Costa Rica, Bella Vista Barracks. Now converted to the showing of national treasures, it features fine exhibits of the artifacts left by prehistoric peoples of the area. There also are exhibits of plant and animal life and many relics of early Costa Rican history. Another museum is the La Salle, featuring mostly natural history collections.

One of the most splendid buildings of the city is the national post office. The stamps of Costa Rica are great favorites of many collectors. Another prominent building is the National Library, also in the downtown section.

Among the most unusual enterprises of any national government is the National Liquor Factory of Costa Rica. This government-owned factory produces a variety of liquors which have gained wide fame. Considered most unusual are the crema de nance and the Cocarí rum.

San José has a large public market on Avenida Central. It is colorful and interesting, though not quite so much so as those of the neighboring countries, since the picturesque clothing and customs of a variety of races are mostly absent. Here is sold almost every kind of fruit and vegetable grown in the torrid and temperate zones, along with the handicrafts of the area.

Until 1957, the University of Costa Rica was located in the heart of San José. It then moved into the new University City in the suburban city of San Pedro de Montes de Oca.

### CARTAGO

Most of the major cities of Costa Rica—Heredia, Alajuela, and Cartago—lie near the capital, nourished by the richness of the Central Valley.

Cartago, about fifteen miles from San José, may be reached by a good, but extremely busy, two-lane highway that is part of the Pan American system. The capital for much of the region's modern life, Cartago has often been scourged by earthquakes but has always sprung back to new and energetic life. Among the most interesting points are the ruins of the old church that was destroyed by earthquake in 1910. A complete contrast is the main market near the railroad station, most colorful on Sunday. From miles around come the people of the country dressed in their Sunday best, a few still driving the colorful oxcarts filled with many kinds of merchandise. Sold here are delicious fruits of every variety, green coffee in sacks, leather goods and other handmade work, vegetables and flowers, and many other more exotic goods.

In Cartago is the Shrine of Our Lady of Angels. The history of the church is very interesting. In 1653 an Indian girl named Mercedes Pereira found a small statue of carved stone placed on a rock. Three times the statue was removed from the rock and taken to a place of safety; each time it disappeared, only to be found on the rock again. The Virgin Mary is said to have appeared three times at the same site near which there was a bubbling spring.

The waters were said to have miraculous powers of healing. A church was built on the site, and the stone image of the Virgin was enshrined in an ornate altar. Over the years the church has come to be considered the most sacred spot in Costa Rica. The feast day of the saint on August 2, the day the Virgin first appeared, is a national holiday. Great crowds of pilgrims from all over Central America and Mexico throng the streets of Cartago. The tiny sacred stone image, called La Negrita because of the dark color of the stone, is solemnly carried from its own church to another church in the city, and then is returned by equally solemn procession.

There are several interesting side trips from Cartago. On the outskirts lies Balneario de Agua Caliente, a tourist resort

Among the most interesting sights in Cartago are the ruins of the colonial church (below) that was destroyed by earthquake in 1910.

PAN AMERICAN UNION

Above: UNESCO'S geophysical observation station at Irazú volcano.
Below: One of two craters at Irazú volcano, one of the major tourist attractions of Central America.

ERNST A. JAHN

ERNST A. JAHN

with hot, spring-fed swimming pools. Nearby factories that make primitive earthen roofing tiles may be seen.

The colorful village of Orosí nestles in the hills near Cartago. Here, more than three hundred years ago, the Spanish built their first mission in Costa Rica; it is still maintained there today. On the banks of the Reventazón River are many popular restaurants and swimming sites.

Close to Orosí lies the beautiful valley of Cachí, known as the "Valley of Enchantment." The road winds around a valley that has been compared by some tourists to the almost unique valleys of Hawaii. Halfway down the valley, dappled with groves of oranges and other citrus fruit, the beautiful Bridal Veil cascade may be seen.

### AWESOME IRAZÚ

Perhaps the most awe-inspiring excursion out of Cartago is a visit to the volcano Irazú. From Cartago one of the most picturesque roads of the hemisphere ascends the side of the volcano in almost constant twists and turns, passing lush dairy land where the cattle graze on such steep slopes that the natives laughingly say they have longer legs on one side than the other.

Irazú has been more or less active since a violent eruption in 1963 and has become one of the major tourist attractions of Central America. The road arrives at a breathtaking halt at more than eleven thousand feet, where a lookout shelter has been built. From this point, visitors must trudge, panting because of the altitude, across the razor sharp lava bed to reach the rim of the crater itself. Here one can look down and see the black walls of the crater that look like the sides of some great furnace from which the fires have just gone out. Most of the time the crater smokes and sometimes has periods of minor activity. The visitor has the eerie feeling that he has entered another world.

In addition to the attraction of Irazú itself, on a clear day both the Pacific and Atlantic oceans can be seen from the mountain's crest.

On the way back to Cartago or San José, most visitors stop at a charming wayside inn, where lunch is served at tables overlooking a vast expanse of Costa Rican countryside.

### OTHER CENTRAL PLATEAU CITIES

The city of Heredia is the capital of the smallest of Costa Rica's seven provinces, and is commonly known as the City of Flowers, "La Ciudad de las Flores." It is also known as the coffee capital of the country. Across the street from Central Park in Heredia is the old Spanish cathedral built in 1787. To the north of the park are the ruins of an old fort.

Founded by Andalusians, this typical Spanish colonial town has the white houses with red tiled roofs and the beautiful patios and towers of colonial times.

Above Heredia towers the volcano Poás; it too can be reached by a paved road. On the way, the road passes the village of Barba, which is known mainly as the birthplace of a former president of the country, Cleto Gonzalez Víquez.

Although Poás is only about nine thousand feet high, it is said to have one of the largest craters in the world. At one time it also had one of the world's largest geysers which shot hot sulphur water out of the center of a small lake. The jet sometimes reached a steaming height of three thousand feet. Suddenly a few years ago the crater shot a shower of ashes up to twenty-three thousand feet; when the air had cleared, the small lake and the geyser had been swallowed up in the great crater, never to reappear.

Nearly a mile from the crater there is a beautiful quiet lake of crystal clear water, nestled in the heart of another old crater.

About eight miles distant from Heredia is the city of Alajuela, capital of Alajuela Province, one of the important communities of Costa Rica. Founded in 1782, one of its most interesting features is Central Park, with its beautiful garden surrounded by enormous mango trees. In Santamaría Park is the statue of the national hero, Juan Santamaría, who fought against the William Walker forces in 1856. Renowned for its climate, the area is popular with tourists; the people of San José especially like to vacation there. It is an important center of cattle raising and sugar production, as well as grain. A picturesque weekly cattle fair is held at Alajuela.

Alajeula Cathedral (below), a famous old church in the capital city of Alajeula Province. Opposite: Near the Spanish colonial town of Heredia, Poás volcano has the largest crater in the world.

NATIONAL TOURIST BUREAU OF COSTA RICA

PAN AMERICAN UNION

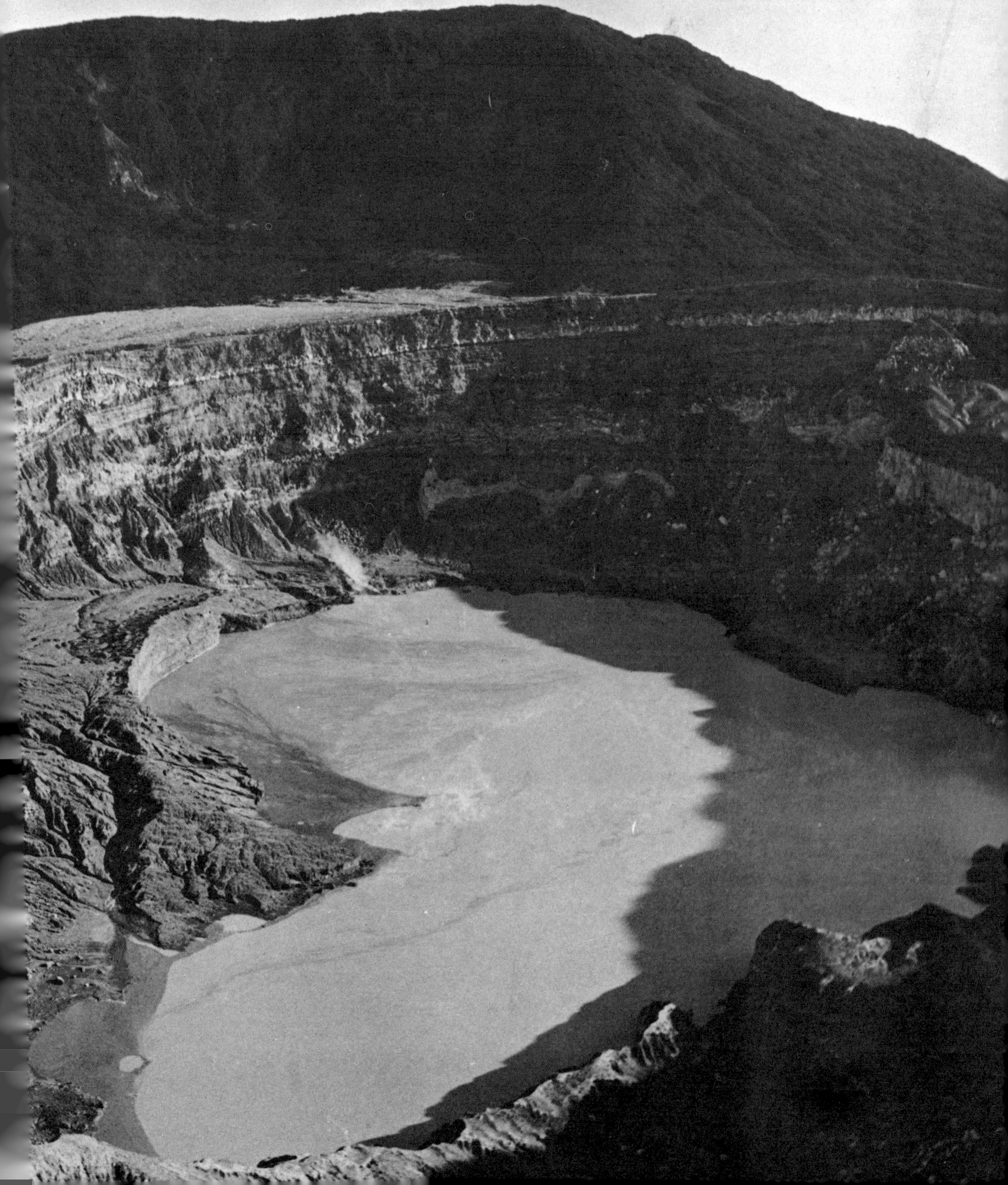

Not far from Alajuela is the swimming resort of Ojo de Agua. Here a very large spring throws out six thousand gallons of water each minute and provides the water supply for the port city of Puntarenas. One of Central America's finest swimming pools and a good restaurant with a dance floor add to the popularity of the resort.

## A NOVEL TRAIN RIDE

By air the trip from San José to the port of Limón takes only about thirty-five minutes. By train it takes at least six hours, but many travelers call the ride the experience of a lifetime.

Pulled by an engine painted a startling orange-red, the narrow-gauge train covers the hundred-mile journey each way twice a day. The train saunters out of San José and winds its way over the Central Valley to cross the mountains. Orchids and other flowers bedeck the steep wall on the train's left. To the right, the brilliant fire-of-the-forest trees spread their bright branches.

When the train pauses at Cartago, visitors are entertained by the vendors, most of them youngsters, who scramble onto the train and try to sell everything from ice cream to scissors. There is no dining car but the vendors offer cold beer and potato chips.

Farther on, the train begins to follow the course of the Reventazón River. Waterfalls add to the spectacular grandeur of the valley's scenery. The tracks slope so steeply that the train goes down no faster than fifteen miles per hour.

As the journey continues, coffee plantations are passed, with an occasional bright painted cart coming into view. As the train passes small communities, most of the residents line the right-of-way to wave and watch the train go by and to be seen themselves. Here most of the people are descendants of the Jamaican workers brought in to build the railroad. As the train drops to lower altitudes, the surroundings become a true tropical jungle. When the train leaves the Reventazón, it crosses several other rivers and then runs along the quiet Rio Blanco. Through groves of coco palm trees the ocean can sometimes be seen, breaking in great noisy waves on lonely beaches.

## PUERTO LIMÓN

At last the train enters Costa Rica's major port city, Limón, another favorite spot for vacationers with its beaches, parks, and the offshore island of Uvita. The city is a main point of departure for the wonderful deep-sea fishing of the Caribbean. The annual National Tarpon Tournament is held at Limón. Nearby, also, are such fishing rivers as the Matina, Mohin, Parismina, and San Juan. Just north of Limón there is good fishing and boating in a region of rivers and lagoons known as Lagunas de Tortuguero. Swimming is delightful at Playa Bonita Beach, until about four o'clock in the afternoon when the sharks arrive.

The city is well lighted and has good streets and excellent sanitation. Among its

The harbor of the Pacific Coast port of Puntarenas.

principal points are the Club Miramor and its popular saltwater pool, the cathedral, the miniature botanical garden of Parque Vargas, and the United Fruit Company zone. Visitors like to watch the loading of bananas at the port. Especially spectacular are the sunsets of Limón.

### OTHER POINTS OF INTEREST

Almost equally interesting to tourists is the Pacific Coast port of Puntarenas. Many consider Puntarenas Province one of the most beautiful of Costa Rica. The city of Puntarenas is the third largest of the nation. Although it is quite warm, it ranks as a favorite summer resort, especially for tourists from the Central Plateau, anxious for the change to sand and salt water. Holiday crowds jam the area from January to March. Puntarenas is known for its fine restaurants, its social and sports clubs, modern stores, abundant fishing, and especially for its wonderful beaches. Though Playas de Jaco, one of the fine beach areas, can be reached only by a rough road, it is a favorite of local beach enthusiasts.

Sightseeing tours can be made from Puntarenas to San Isidro, El Roble, Boca de Barranca, Doña Ana, Mata de Limón,

Aerial view of Golfito, a Pacific Coast port with many fine beaches.

UNITED FRUIT COMPANY

as well as to the islands of Venado, Tortugas, Cedros, and Negritos.

The other major Pacific port, Golfito, is a picturesque town with many attractions for tourists, including many fine beaches, but it has not yet been developed to accommodate many visitors.

One of the most spectacular stretches of the Pan American Highway in all of Central America is that part which follows Talamanca Ridge in Costa Rica. Here it winds for about ten miles over the crest of the ridge, sometimes offering extraordinary views of the Atlantic and the Pacific.

### TREASURE ISLAND

Some of the islands off the Pacific shore are known for typical tourist attractions, especially the very good beaches of El

Coro and San Lucas Island, site of the famous liberal prison of Costa Rica.

Not a typical tourist attraction, however, is Cocos Island, where more than five hundred separate expeditions have vainly dug for buried treasure. There are many interesting legends about the reputed wealth. Perhaps the most popular is the story of the hidden golden Virgin of Peru. According to the story, some of the people of Peru who had joined the revolution against Spain chartered the ship the *Mary Dyer* and attempted to escape the Spanish forces. According to the legend, they carried with them amazing quantities of the vast treasures of Peru. When pursued by a Spanish warship, the people are believed to have fled to Cocos Island and buried most of the treasure before the Spaniards caught up with them. This treasure has never been found. The most fabulous piece of this treasure was reputed to be a lifesize solid gold statue of the Virgin Mary.

Another of the treasure stories concerns the pirate William Dampier. In 1684 he blockaded Panama and captured a number of ships that were hauling off the treasures of Peru. He is said to have hidden much of this treasure on Cocos Island.

Still another treasure legend is that during the revolutionary times in Latin America, citizens of Costa Rica loaded several ships with jewels, silver, gold, and other treasure and buried it all on Cocos. Only six men are supposed to have known the location, and they all died before it could be recovered. This is the least likely of all, since little of such great wealth was known in Costa Rica.

All visitors to the island must have government permission, and permits are required for treasure hunting. The hunter agrees to divide his find equally with the government, but so far no one has made a lucky strike of the estimated 100 million dollar horde.

Countless weary treasure seekers have succumbed to the aches of shoulders and back, tired of digging, without any success. Luckier are the treasure seekers who go to Cocos looking only for the wonderful scenery and game fish. One of these who visited the island several times was United States President Franklin D. Roosevelt.

Fortunately, Costa Rica does not have to depend on any mythical treasure. The riches of its soils and the character of its people are wealth enough.

# Handy Reference Section

## INSTANT FACTS

*Political:*
Official Name—Republic of Costa Rica
Capital—San José
Monetary Unit—Colón
Official Language—Spanish
Independence Day—September 15
National Heroes—Juan Rafael Mora and Juan Santamaría
National Flag—Two blue horizontal stripes, top and bottom; two white inner stripes; and a wider red center band on which appears the country's coat of arms. The blue and white colors are derived from the flag adopted in 1823 by the United Provinces of Central America.
National Shield—A shield with a ribbon at the top representing Central America, below another ribbon with words Republica de Costa Rica; in center of shield mountains rise from lush countryside; oceans with ships in foreground and background; the sun is rising, and seven stars represent the seven provinces of Costa Rica.
National Flower—Guaria Morada orchid

*Geographical:*
Area—19,570 square miles
Highest Point—Mount Chirripó Grande, 12,530 feet
Lowest Point—Sea Level

*Population:*
National Population—1,639,980 (1968)
Population Density—28 persons per square mile
Population Distribution—European or mostly European, 98.38%
Negro, 1.60%
Amerindian, .02%
Population Growth Rate—4.2% annually
Birth Rate per 1,000—40.5
Death Rate per 1,000—8.1

## PRINCIPAL CITIES

| | |
|---|---|
| San José | 192,145 |
| Alajuela | 27,305 |
| Puntarenas | 22,545 |
| Heredia | 22,345 |
| Cartago | 20,936 |

## PROVINCES AND CAPITALS

Alajuela—Alajuela
Cartago—Cartago
Guanacaste—Liberia
Heredia—Heredia
Limón—Limón
Puntarenas—Puntarenas
San José—San José

## FIESTAS AND FAIRS

March 19—San José's Day (patron saint of San José)
August—Fiesta of Our Lady of the Angels (La Negrita)—entire country but especially Cartago
August 15—The Assumption and Mother's Day, entire country
September 15—Independence Day, entire country
October 12—Columbus Day, entire country
October—Halloween, San José
November 3—All Souls' Day, entire country
December 8—Immaculate Conception, entire country
December 24-January 1—Popular Fiestas, San José

## YOU HAVE A DATE WITH HISTORY

1502—Columbus discovers Costa Rica
1522—Spanish explore Pacific Coast; Bruselas founded
1564—Don Juan Vasquéz de Coronado founds Cartago, first permanent settlement
1717—Heredia founded
1737—San José founded
1808—Coffee first introduced
1821—Spanish rule ends
1822—Mexico claims control
1823—Costa Rica joins United Provinces of Central America; Cartago destroyed; capital moved to San José
1825—First constitution adopted, within the framework of United Provinces of Central America
1838—United Provinces of Central America dissolved
1842—Braulio Carrillo forced from office; Francisco Morazán takes over; Morazán executed
1848—Costa Rica proclaims itself a republic
1850—Spain finally recognizes Costa Rican independence
1856—Juan Rafael Mora routs William Walker, aided by Juan Santamaría

91

1878—Costa Rica is first Central American country to raise bananas commercially
1889—New constitution established; first free elections held
1890—Railroad completed from San José to Limón
1909—Railroad completed from San José to Puntarenas
1917—Coup d'état of Federico Tinoco
1949—Present constitution put into effect; army abolished
1960—Foreign ministers of Organization of American States meet in San José
1965—National Theater declared a national monument
1970—José Figueres becomes president of Costa Rica

## SPANISH PRONUNCIATION GUIDE

Abajonel (ah vah ho NEL)
Alajuela (ah lah HWE lah)
Arenal (ah reh NAHL)
Atlanta (ah TLAHN tah)
Balneario de Agua Caliente (bahl neh AH ryo deh ah gwah kah LYEN teh)
Bananito (bah nah NEE toh)
Bruselas (broo SEH lahs)
Burica (boo REE kah)
Caldera (kahl DEH rah)
Caño Bravo (kah nyo BRAH vo)
Cartago (kahr TAH go)
Chirripó Grande (chee ree POH GRAHN deh)
Cordillera Central (kor dee YAY rah sen TRAHL)
Cucaracha (koo kah RAH cha)
Doña Ana (doh nya AH nah)
Golfito (gohl FEE toh)
Grande de Tárcoles (GRAHN deh deh TAHR koh lehs)
Grande de Térraba (GRAHN deh deh TEH rah vah)
Guanacaste (gwah nah KAHS teh)
Guápiles (GWAH pee lehs)
Heredia (eh REH dyah)
Irazú (ee rah SOO)
Liberia (lee VEH ryah)
Limón (lee MOHN)
Monteverde de Guacimal (mohn teh VEHR deh deh gwah see MAHL)
Negritos (neh GREE tohs)
Nicoya (nee KOH yah)
Ojo de Agua (oh ho deh AH gwah)
Poás (poh AHS)
Portete (pohr TEH teh)
Puerto Cortés (pwehr toh kohr TEHS)
Punta Cahuila (puhn tah kah WEE lah)
Puntarenas (poon tah REH nahs)
Reventazón (reh vehn tah SOHN)
San José (sahn ho SEH)
San Pedro de Montes de Oca (sahn PEH droh deh mohn tehs deh OH kah)
Tempisque (tehm PEES keh)
Tortuguero (tohr too GEH roh)
Turrialba (too RYAHL bah)
Ujarrás (oo hah RAHS)
Venecia de San Carlos (beh NEH sya deh sahn KAHR lohs)
Volcán (bohl KAHN)

asada (ah SAH dah)
Avenida Central (ah veh NEE dah sehn TRAHL)
chirimía (chee ree MEE ah)
hacienda (ah SYEHN dah)
Josefino (ho seh FEE noh)
Paseo Colón (pah SEH oh koh LOHN)
punto guanasteco (POON toh gwah nah kahs TEH koh)
quijongo (kee HOHN goh)
Coronado, Juan Vasqúez de (koh roh NAH doh, HWAHN BAHS kehs deh)

Echandi, Enrique (eh CHAHN dee ehn REE keh)
Echeverria, Aquileo (eh che veh REE ah, ah kee LEH oh)
Figueres, José (Don Pepe) (fee GEH rehs, ho SEH) (dohn PEH peh)
Iturbide, Agustín (ee toor BEE deh, ah goos TEEN)
Morazán, Francisco (moh rah SAHN, frahn SEES koh)
Santamaría, Juan (sahn tah mah REE ah, HWAHN)

# Index

Abajonel Hill, 54
Agriculture, 65, 66
Agüero, Arturo, 45
Airports, 71
Alajuela (city), 37, 46, 66, 71, 74, 84
Alajuela Province, 15, 54, 84
Amighetti, Francisco, 42
Animals, 54
Arenal (volcano), 11
Arenal Lake, 14
Art, prehistoric, 17, 29, 31
Artists, 42, 45
Asada (barbecue), 20, 62
Atlanta, 74
Avenida Central, San José, 77, 80
Aviation, 71

Bakit, Oscar, 45
Balneario de Agua Caliente, 81
Bananas, 39, 65
Bananito River, 14
Banano River, 14
Barba, 84
Barbecue (asada), 20, 62
Barrade Colorado, 70
Bauxite, 54

Berthaud, Margarita, 45
Birds, 54
Blanco River, 14, 86
Bolívar Park, San José, 78
Bolson, 70
Bonilla, Abelardo, 45
Bonilla, Juan Ramón, 76
Boruca people, 31, 56
Bruselas, 32
Bulgarelli, Pietro, 76
Bullfighting, 21, 62

Cachí Valley, 83
Caldera, 70
Caño Bravo River, 14
Caño Island, 56
Cariari, 31
Caribbean Sea, 12
Carrillo, Braulio, 35, 36
Cartago, 15, 21, 25, 32, 34, 41, 80, 81, 86
Carts, ox, 21, 22, 62, 75
Cathedral of San José, 18, 78
Central Park, San José, 25, 78
Central Range, 14
Central Valley, 14, 15, 32, 34, 46, 60, 65, 66, 73
Chacón, Juan Rafael, 42

Chichicastenango, Guatemala, 18
Chilito River, 14
Chiquero River, 14
Chira Island, 12
Chorotega tribe, 31
Climate, 15
Coastlines, 12
Cocos Island, 12, 89
Coffee, 38, 65
College of San Luis Gonzaga, 50
Colorado River, 14
Columbus, Christopher, 31, 77
Communications, 74
Conservative Party, 36
Constitutions, 35, 38, 41, 45, 61
Continental Divide, 12, 17
Cordillera Central, 11, 14
Coris, 21, 66
Coronado, Don Juan Vásquez de, 32
Coronado Bay, 14
Costumbrismo, 27, 45
Cóter Lake, 14
Cowboys, 20, 63
Creamuno, Julio Mata, 45
Crops, 65, 66
Cucaracha River, 14

Dampier, William, 89
Dance, national, 20, 58
Deel, Luis, 45
Dobles, Fabian, 45
Duffner, Raúl Cabezas, 45
Duran, 26, 61

Earthquakes, 34, 41, 80
Echandi, Enrique, 42
Echeverria, Aquileo J., 45
Education, 46-50
El Coco Airport, 18, 71, 75
El Coro Island, 89
El Congo Hill, 54
El Enano (The Dwarf), 18, 42
El Salvador, 18
Erizo (the Hedgehog), 37
Escuela de Tejidos, 46
Ethnic backgrounds, 58
Exports, 69, 70

Federation of Central America, 34
Fernández, Lola, 45
Fiestas, 21, 62
Figueres Ferrer, José, 18, 41, 42

94

Fish, 20, 54, 86
Flor, Juan López de la, 32
Flower, national, 54
Fonseca, Harold, 45
Forests, 53, 69
Frio River, 14

Garita, Father Juan, 27, 45
Geography, 10-14
Geology, 15
Gold, 29, 31
Golfito, 70, 74, 88
González, Alfredo, 41
González, Hernán, 42
González, Manuel de la Cruz, 45
González Víquez, Cleto, 84
Government, 45, 46
Guacalito River, 14
Guacimo, 54
Guanacaste, El, tree, 54
Guanacaste Province, 19, 20, 31, 37, 53, 54, 57, 62, 69
Guanacaste Range, 11, 20
Guardia, Tomás, 38
Guaria morada orchid, 54
Guatemala, 34
Guatemala City, 18, 34
Guayacán tree, 53
Güetare tribe, 31
Gulf of Nicoya, 11, 12, 14, 61, 69
Gutiérrez, Julio Fonseca, 45

Haciendas River, 14
Health, 21, 26, 60, 61
Heredia, 34, 50, 65, 83
Highways, 71, 73
Honduras, 18

Iglesias, Rafael, 7
Imports, 69
Income, annual per person, 60
Independence, 34, 36
Indians, 29, 31, 56, 57, 58
Industry, 68, 69
Inner Arch (central mountains), 15
Inter-American Institute of Agricultural Science, 26, 50

Irazú (volcano), 11, 25, 26, 83
Islands, 12, 89
Iturbide, Agustin, 34

Jaffe, William, 31
Jaguars, 54
Jiménez, Max, 45
Johnson, Lyndon B. 11, 18, 42
Josefinos, 16, 62

Keith, Minor Cooper, 26, 39
Kennedy, John F., 10, 42

Lagunas de Tortuguero, 86
Lake Nicaragua, 14, 18
Lakes, 14
Languages, 26, 46
La Sabana Airport, 71, 77
Las Concavas, 66
Legislative Assembly, 41, 45, 46, 80
Liberal Party, 36
Liberia, 19, 50
Limón (city), 18, 26, 31, 39, 53, 70, 71, 73, 74, 86
Limón Basin, 15
Limón Province, 26, 54, 60
Limón River, 14
Linea Vieja, 31
Literacy rate, 46
Livestock, 66
Lottery, National, 78
Luján, Flora, 45

Machado, Guillermo Aguilar, 45
Madre de Dios River, 14
Manufacturing, 68, 69
Matina River, 14, 86
Mena River, 14
Merced Park, San José, 29, 78
Mesén, Roberto Brenes, 45
Mexico, 34
Minerals, 54, 56, 69
Ministry of Public Health, 60
Mohin River, 86
Monestel, Alejandro, 45

Monteverde de Guacinial, 62
Mora, Argüello, 27, 45
Mora, Juan Rafael, 37
Morazán, Francisco, 35, 36
Morazán Park, San José 78
Mountains, 11, 15
Mount Chiropó Grande, 11
Music, 45
Musical instruments, 21, 63

National Conservatory of Music, 45
National Liquor Factory, 80
National Museum, 17, 25, 80
National Park, San José, 78
National Theater, 7, 8, 25, 42, 76
Navarro, 66
Negrita, La, 25, 81
Negroes, 18, 26, 60
Newspapers, 74
Nicaragua, 14, 17, 36, 38, 70
Nicoya Gulf, 11, 12, 14, 61, 69
Nicoya Peninsula, 11, 12, 14, 15, 32, 73
Nieto, César A., 45
Nixon, Richard M., 42

Ojo de Agua, 68, 86
Organization of American States, 42, 50
Orosí, 83
Osa Peninsula, 12
Outer Arch (Pacific Coast), 15
Oxcarts, 21, 22, 62, 75

Pacific Ocean, 12
Pacuare River, 14
Palacios River, 14
Panama, 12, 14, 73
Panama City, 17, 73
Pan American Highway, 11, 17, 73, 88
Paraiso, 21, 66
Parismina River, 14, 86

Paris Opera Company, 7
Paseo Colón, San José, 77
Peña, Alfredo Cardona, 45
Pereira, Mercedes, 81
Pirates, 32, 89
Pizote River, 14
Playas del Coco, 20
Playas de Jaco, 87
Poás (volcano), 11, 12, 84
Podevano, Tomás, 42
Point Burica, 12
Population figures, 14, 60
Portete, 32
Ports, 69, 70
Portugues, Juan, 45
Prisons, 61, 89
Punta Cahuila, 70
Puntarenas (city), 18, 32, 39, 41, 69, 73, 74, 86, 87
Puntarenas Province, 54, 69, 87

Quepos, 70
Quirós, Federico, 45

Railroads, 26, 39, 73, 74
Rainfall, 15
Ranches, 19
Religion, 62
Retreta, 63
Reventazón River, 14, 39, 83, 86
Rio Grande de Tárcoles, 14
Rio Grande de Térraba, 14, 56
Rio General Valley, 54
Rio Pirris, 14
Rivas, 37
Rivers, 14, 70
Roads, 71, 73
Rockefeller, Nelson A., 42
Roman Catholicism, 62
Roosevelt, Franklin D., 89

Salazar, Manuel, 45
San Carlos River, 14
Sanchez, Juan Manuel, 42
San Isidro, 73
San José, (city) 15, 16-18, 23, 25, 26, 29, 34, 39, 41, 46, 50, 62, 63, 68, 71, 73, 74, 75-80, 86
San José Province, 54
San Juan River, 14, 86
San Lucas Island, 61, 89

95

San Pedro de Montes de Oca, 50, 80
San Ramón, 50
Santamaría, Juan, 37, 84
Sapoa River, 14
Sarapiquí River, 14
School of Special Instruction, 46
Schools, 46-50
Shrine of Our Lady of Angels, 25, 81
Sixaola River, 14
Social Security Agency, 46
Spanish in Costa Rica, 32, 34, 57
Sports, 63

Supreme Court of Justice, 46

Talamanca Range, 11, 14, 17, 88
Telephones, 74
Temperatures, 15
Tempisque River, 14, 70
Ticos, 62
Tinoco, Federico, 41
Toro Amarillo, 74
Torres, Rafael Chávez, 45
Tortuguero River, 14
Transportation, 69-74
Tree, national, 54

Trees, 53, 54, 69
Trejos Fernández, José Joaquín, 42
Turrialba (city), 26, 50
Turrialba (volcano), 12

Ujarrás, 34
Ulate Blanco, Otilio, 41
United Fruit Company, 39, 70, 87
United Provinces of Central America, 35
University of Costa Rica, 18, 50, 80
Uvita Island, 86

Valverde, César, 45
Venecia de San Carlos, 54
Vignani, Luigi, 76
Villa, José, 76
Volcanoes, 10-12, 15, 25, 83, 84

Walker, William, 36-38
Willie, Emilio, 45
Writers, 27, 45

Zapote River, 14
Zeledón, Paco, 42
Zuñiga, Daniel, 45

96